MznLnx

Missing Links Exam Preps

Exam Prep for

Microeconomics

Pindyck & Rubinfeld, 6th Edition

The MznLnx Exam Prep is your link from the texbook and lecture to your exams.
The MznLnx Exam Preps are unauthorized and comprehensive reviews of your textbooks.

MznLnx

Rico
Publications

Exam Prep for Microeconomics
6th Edition
Pindyck & Rubinfeld

Publisher: Raymond Houge

Assistant Editor: Michael Rouger

Text and Cover Designer: Lisa Buckner

Marketing Manager: Sara Swagger

Project Manager, Editorial Production: Jerry Emerson

Art Director: Vernon Lowerui

Product Manager: Dave Mason

Editorial Assitant: Rachel Guzmanji

Pedagogy: Debra Long

Cover Image: Jim Reed/Getty Images

Text and Cover Printer: City Printing, Inc.

Compositor: Media Mix, Inc.

For more information about our products, contact us at:

Dave.Mason@RicoPublications.com

For permission to use material from this text or

product, submit a request online to:

Dave.Mason@RicoPublications.com

Printed in the United States
ISBN:

Contents

TO THE STUDENT

COMPREHENSIVE

The *MznLnx* Exam Prep series is designed to help you pass your exams. Editors at MznLnx review your textbooks and then prepare these practice exams to help you master the textbook material. Unlike study guides, workbooks, and practice tests provided by the texbook publisher and textbook authors, *MznLnx* gives you **all** of the material in each chapter in exam form, not just samples, so you can be sure to nail your exam.

MECHANICAL

The MznLnx Exam Prep series creates exams that will help you learn the subject matter as well as test you on your understanding. Each question is designed to help you master the concept. Just working through the exams, you gain an understanding of the subject--its a simple mechanical process that produces success.

INTEGRATED STUDY GUIDE AND REVIEW

MznLnx is not just a set of exams designed to test you, its also a comprehensive review of the subject content. Each exam question is also a review of the concept, making sure that you will get the answer correct without having to go to other sources of material. You learn as you go! Its the easiest way to pass an exam.

HUMOR

Studying can be tedious and dry. MznLnx's instructional design includes moderate humor within the exam questions on occassion, to break the tedium and revitalize the brain

1. _____ is a branch of economics that deals with the performance, structure, and behavior of a national or regional economy as a whole. Along with microeconomics, _____ is one of the two most general fields in economics. It is the study of the behavior and decision-making of entire economies.
   a. New Trade Theory
   c. Tobit model

   b. Nominal value
   d. Macroeconomics

2. _____ is a branch of economics that studies how individuals, households and firms and some states make decisions to allocate limited resources, typically in markets where goods or services are being bought and sold. _____ examines how these decisions and behaviours affect the supply and demand for goods and services, which determines prices; and how prices, in turn , determine the supply and demand of goods and services.

   Whereas macroeconomics involves the 'sum total of economic activity, dealing with the issues of growth, inflation and unemployment, and with national economic policies relating to these issues' and the effects of government actions on them.

   a. Recession
   c. Countercyclical

   b. Microeconomics
   d. New Keynesian economics

3. _____ is a broad label that refers to any individuals or households that use goods and services generated within the economy. The concept of a _____ is used in different contexts, so that the usage and significance of the term may vary.

   Typically when business people and economists talk of _____s they are talking about person as _____, an aggregated commodity item with little individuality other than that expressed in the buy/not-buy decision.

   a. 130-30 fund
   c. 100-year flood

   b. 1921 recession
   d. Consumer

4. _____ is the study of when, why, how, where and what people do or do not buy products. It blends elements from psychology, sociology,social psychology, anthropology and economics. It attempts to understand the buyer decision making process, both individually and in groups.
   a. Shopping Neutral
   c. Consumption smoothing

   b. Situational theory of publics
   d. Consumer behavior

5. A _____ is a situation that involves losing one quality or aspect of something in return for gaining another quality or aspect. It implies a decision to be made with full comprehension of both the upside and downside of a particular choice.

   In economics the term is expressed as opportunity cost, referring the most preferred alternative given up.

   a. Whitemail
   c. Nonmarket

   b. Friedman-Savage utility function
   d. Trade-off

6. A _____ or directed economy is an economic system in which the government or workers' councils manages the economy. It is an economic system in which the central government makes all decisions on the production and consumption of goods and services. Its most extensive form is referred to as a command economy, centrally _____, or command and control economy.

a. Dual economy

b. Network economics

c. Planned economy

d. Closed economy

7. In microeconomics, _____ is quite simply the conversion of inputs into outputs. It is an economic process that uses resources to create a good or service that is suitable for exchange. This can include manufacturing, storing, shipping, and packaging.

a. Red Guards

b. MET

c. Solved

d. Production

8. _____ in economics and business is the result of an exchange and from that trade we assign a numerical monetary value to a good, service or asset. If Alice trades Bob 4 apples for an orange, the _____ of an orange is 4 apples. Inversely, the _____ of an apple is 1/4 oranges.

a. Price book

b. Price

c. Premium pricing

d. Price war

9. The _____ consists of a number of economic theories which describe the nature of the firm, company including its existence, its behaviour, and its relationship with the market.

In simplified terms, the _____ aims to answer these questions:

1. Existence - why do firms emerge, why are not all transactions in the economy mediated over the market?
2. Boundaries - why the boundary between firms and the market is located exactly there? Which transactions are performed internally and which are negotiated on the market?
3. Organization - why are firms structured in such specific way? What is the interplay of formal and informal relationships?

Despite looking simple, these questions are not answered by the established economic theory, which usually views firms as given, and treats them as black boxes without any internal structure.

The First World War period saw a change of emphasis in economic theory away from industry-level analysis which mainly included analysing markets to analysis at the level of the firm, as it became increasingly clear that perfect competition was no longer an adequate model of how firms behaved. Economic theory till then had focussed on trying to understand markets alone and there had been little study on understanding why firms or organisations exist.

a. Policy Ineffectiveness Proposition

b. Theory of the firm

c. Technology gap

d. Khazzoom-Brookes postulate

10. _____s is concerned with the tasks of developing and applying quantitative or statistical methods to the study and elucidation of economic principles. _____s combines economic theory with statistics to analyze and test economic relationships. Theoretical _____s considers questions about the statistical properties of estimators and tests, while applied _____s is concerned with the application of _____ methods to assess economic theories.

a. Econometric

b. Experimental economics

c. Economic

d. Evolutionary economics

11. In economics and finance, _____ is the practice of taking advantage of a price differential between two or more markets: striking a combination of matching deals that capitalize upon the imbalance, the profit being the difference between the market prices. When used by academics, an _____ is a transaction that involves no negative cash flow at any probabilistic or temporal state and a positive cash flow in at least one state; in simple terms, a risk-free profit. A person who engages in _____ is called an arbitrageur--such as a bank or brokerage firm.

a. Arbitrage

b. Electronic trading

c. Alternext

d. Options Price Reporting Authority

12. A _____ is a counterfeit agreement among industries. It is an informal organization of producers that agree to coordinate prices and production. _____s usually occur in an oligopolistic industry, where there is a small number of sellers and usually involve homogeneous products.

a. Cartel

b. Shill

c. 100-year flood

d. Shanzhai

13. _____ is an economic concept with commonplace familiarity. It is the price that a good or service is offered at, or will fetch, in the marketplace. It is of interest mainly in the study of microeconomics.

a. Paper trading

b. Noisy market hypothesis

c. Market anomaly

d. Market price

14. The Organization of the Petroleum Exporting Countries is a cartel of twelve countries made up of Algeria, Angola, Ecuador, Iran, Iraq, Kuwait, Libya, Nigeria, Qatar, Saudi Arabia, the United Arab Emirates, and Venezuela. The cartel has maintained its headquarters in Vienna since 1965, and hosts regular meetings among the oil ministers of its Member Countries. Indonesia withdrew its membership in _____ in 2008 after it became a net importer of oil, but stated it would likely return if it became a net exporter in the world.

a. ACCRA Cost of Living Index

b. AD-IA Model

c. ACEA agreement

d. OPEC

15. In political science and economics, the _____ or agency dilemma treats the difficulties that arise under conditions of incomplete and asymmetric information when a principal hires an agent, such as the problem that the two may not have the same interests, while the principal is, presumably, hiring the agent to pursue the interests of the former.

Various mechanisms may be used to try to align the interests of the agent with those of the principal, such as piece rates/commissions, profit sharing, efficiency wages, performance measurement (including financial statements), the agent posting a bond, or fear of firing. The _____ is found in most employer/employee relationships, for example, when stockholders hire top executives of corporations.

a. Principal-agent problem

b. 100-year flood

c. 1921 recession

d. 130-30 fund

16. _____ is a common concept in economics, and gives rise to derived concepts such as consumer debt. Generally _____ is defined by opposition to production. But the precise definition can vary because different schools of economists define production quite differently.

a. Cash or share options

b. Consumption

c. Foreclosure data providers

d. Federal Reserve Bank Notes

17. The term _____ or commodity bundle refers to a fixed list of items used specifically to track the progress of inflation in an economy or specific market.

The most common type of _____ is the basket of consumer goods, used to define the Consumer Price Index (CPI.) Other types of baskets are used to define

- Producer Price Index (PPI), previously known as Wholesale Price Index (WPI)
- various commodity price indices

The term _____ analysis in the retail business refers to research that provides the retailer with information to understand the purchase behaviour of a buyer. This information will enable the retailer to understand the buyer's needs and rewrite the store's layout accordingly, develop cross-promotional programs, or even capture new buyers (much like the cross-selling concept.)

a. Category Development Index

b. Cost-weighted activity index

c. Robin Hood index

d. Market basket

18. Economics:

- _____ ,the desire to own something and the ability to pay for it
- _____ curve,a graphic representation of a _____ schedule
- _____ deposit, the money in checking accounts
- _____ pull theory,the theory that inflation occurs when _____ for goods and services exceeds existing supplies
- _____ schedule,a table that lists the quantity of a good a person will buy it each different price
- _____ side economics,the school of economics at believes government spending and tax cuts open economy by raising _____

a. Variability

b. Production

c. McKesson ' Robbins scandal

d. Demand

19. _____ describes a deliberate attempt to interfere with the free and fair operation of the market and create artificial, false or misleading appearances with respect to the price of a security, commodity or currency. _____ is prohibited under Section 9(a)(2) of the Securities Exchange Act of 1934, and in Australia under Section s 1041A of the Corporations Act 2001. The Act defines _____ as transactions which create an artificial price or maintain an artificial price for a tradable security.

a. Managerial economics

b. Net domestic product

c. Legal monopoly

d. Market manipulation

20. In economics, _____ is a measure of the relative satisfaction from consumption of various goods and services. Given this measure, one may speak meaningfully of increasing or decreasing _____, and thereby explain economic behavior in terms of attempts to increase one's _____. For illustrative purposes, changes in _____ are sometimes expressed in units called utils.

a. Expected utility hypothesis

b. Utility function

c. Utility

d. Ordinal utility

21. _____ was a survey conducted by the U.S. Department of Justice to gauge the prevalence of alcohol and illegal drug use among prior arrestees. It was a reformulation of the prior Drug Use Forecasting (DUF) program, focused on five drugs in particular: cocaine, marijuana, methamphetamine, opiates, and PCP.

Participants were randomly selected from arrest records in major metropolitan areas; because no personally identifying information is taken from each record chosen, the resulting data can be correlated to arrest rates, but not to the total population of persons charged.

a. AD-IA Model

b. ACCRA Cost of Living Index

c. ACEA agreement

d. Arrestee Drug Abuse Monitoring

22. Competition law, known in the United States as _____ law, has three main elements:

- prohibiting agreements or practices that restrict free trading and competition between business entities. This includes in particular the repression of cartels.
- banning abusive behaviour by a firm dominating a market, or anti-competitive practices that tend to lead to such a dominant position. Practices controlled in this way may include predatory pricing, tying, price gouging, refusal to deal, and many others.
- supervising the mergers and acquisitions of large corporations, including some joint ventures. Transactions that are considered to threaten the competitive process can be prohibited altogether, or approved subject to 'remedies' such as an obligation to divest part of the merged business or to offer licences or access to facilities to enable other businesses to continue competing.

The substance and practice of competition law varies from jurisdiction to jurisdiction. Protecting the interests of consumers (consumer welfare) and ensuring that entrepreneurs have an opportunity to compete in the market economy are often treated as important objectives. Competition law is closely connected with law on deregulation of access to markets, state aids and subsidies, the privatisation of state owned assets and the establishment of independent sector regulators. In recent decades, competition law has been viewed as a way to provide better public services.

a. Intellectual property law

b. United Kingdom competition law

c. Anti-Inflation Act

d. Antitrust

23. The _____ is responsible for enforcing the antitrust laws of the United States. It shares jurisdiction over civil antitrust cases with the Federal Trade Commission (FTC) and often works jointly with the FTC to provide regulatory guidance to businesses. However, the Antitrust Division also has the power to file criminal cases against willful violators of the antitrust laws.

a. Antitrust

b. Intellectual property law

c. Ease of Doing Business Index

d. United States Department of Justice Antitrust Division

24. The _____, a unit of the United States Department of Labor, is the principal fact-finding agency for the U.S. government in the broad field of labor economics and statistics. The BLS is an independent national statistical agency that collects, processes, analyzes, and disseminates essential statistical data to the American public, the U.S. Congress, other Federal agencies, State and local governments, business, and labor representatives. The BLS also serves as a statistical resource to the Department of Labor.

   a. Gross world product   b. Bureau of Labor Statistics

   c. Gross Regional Product   d. Gross national product

25. A _____ is a measure of the average price of consumer goods and services purchased by households. A _____ measures a price change for a constant market basket of goods and services from one period to the next within the same area (city, region, or nation.) It is a price index determined by measuring the price of a standard group of goods meant to represent the typical market basket of a typical urban consumer.

   a. Lipstick index   b. Cost-of-living index

   c. CPI   d. Consumer Price Index

26. A _____ is a normalized average (typically a weighted average) of prices for a given class of goods or services in a given region, during a given interval of time. It is a statistic designed to help to compare how these prices, taken as a whole, differ between time periods or geographical locations.

Price indices have several potential uses.

   a. Two-part tariff   b. Transactional Net Margin Method

   c. Price Index   d. Product sabotage

27. A _____ is the lowest hourly, daily or monthly wage that employers may legally pay to employees or workers. Equivalently, it is the lowest wage at which workers may sell their labor. Although _____ laws are in effect in a great many jurisdictions, there are differences of opinion about the benefits and drawbacks of a _____.

   a. Permanent war economy   b. Microfoundations

   c. Marginal propensity to consume   d. Minimum wage

28. The _____ is about the attempts and measures governments have made to introduce a standard amount of periodic pay below which employers could not let their workers fall.

In 1824 in Victoria, Australia, an amendment to the Factories Act provided for the creation of a wages board. The wages board did not set a universal minimum wage; rather it set basic wages for 6 industries that were considered to pay low wages.

   a. Council of Economic Advisers   b. Controlled Foreign Corporations

   c. Foreclosure data providers   d. History of Minimum wage

29. The term surplus is used in economics for several related quantities. The consumer surplus is the amount that consumers benefit by being able to purchase a product for a price that is less than they would be willing to pay. The _____ is the amount that producers benefit by selling at a market price mechanism that is higher than they would be willing to sell for.

a. Long term

b. Returns to scale

c. Producer Surplus

d. Schedule delay

1. _____ is a term from economics referring to the use of money exchanged by buyers and sellers with an open and understood system of value and time trade offs to produce the best distribution of goods and services. The use of the _____ does not imply a free market: there can be captive or controlled markets which seek to use supply and demand, or some other form of charging for scarcity, both in social situations and in engineering.

The _____ assumes perfect competition and is regulated by demand and supply.

a. Two-sided markets
c. Partial equilibrium

b. Market mechanism
d. Product-Market Growth Matrix

2. Economics:

- _____,the desire to own something and the ability to pay for it
- _____ curve,a graphic representation of a _____ schedule
- _____ deposit, the money in checking accounts
- _____ pull theory,the theory that inflation occurs when _____ for goods and services exceeds existing supplies
- _____ schedule,a table that lists the quantity of a good a person will buy it each different price
- _____ side economics,the school of economics at believes government spending and tax cuts open economy by raising _____

.

a. Variability
c. McKesson ' Robbins scandal

b. Production
d. Demand

3. In economics, the _____ can be defined as the graph depicting the relationship between the price of a certain commodity, and the amount of it that consumers are willing and able to purchase at that given price. It is a graphic representation of a demand schedule. The _____ for all consumers together follows from the _____ of every individual consumer: the individual demands at each price are added together.

a. Wage curve
c. Cost curve

b. Demand curve
d. Kuznets curve

4. In economics, the concept of the _____ refers to the decision-making time frame of a firm in which at least one factor of production is fixed. Costs which are fixed in the _____ have no impact on a firms decisions. For example a firm can raise output by increasing the amount of labour through overtime.

a. Productivity model
c. Short-run

b. Hicks-neutral technical change
d. Product Pipeline

5. In economics, economic equilibrium is simply a state of the world where economic forces are balanced and in the absence of external influences the (equilibrium) values of economic variables will not change. It is the point at which quantity demanded and quantity supplied are equal. _____, for example, refers to a condition where a market price is established through competition such that the amount of goods or services sought by buyers is equal to the amount of goods or services produced by sellers.

a. Product-Market Growth Matrix
c. Regulated market

b. Market equilibrium
d. Marketization

6. _____ in economics and business is the result of an exchange and from that trade we assign a numerical monetary value to a good, service or asset. If Alice trades Bob 4 apples for an orange, the _____ of an orange is 4 apples. Inversely, the _____ of an apple is 1/4 oranges.

a. Price war

b. Price book

c. Premium pricing

d. Price

7. _____ is a broad label that refers to any individuals or households that use goods and services generated within the economy. The concept of a _____ is used in different contexts, so that the usage and significance of the term may vary.

Typically when business people and economists talk of _____s they are talking about person as _____, an aggregated commodity item with little individuality other than that expressed in the buy/not-buy decision.

a. 100-year flood

b. 1921 recession

c. 130-30 fund

d. Consumer

8. In mathematics, an _____ is a statement about the relative size or order of two objects, or about whether they are the same or not

- The notation a < b means that a is less than b.
- The notation a > b means that a is greater than b.
- The notation a ≠ b means that a is not equal to b, but does not say that one is greater than the other or even that they can be compared in size.

In each statement above, a is not equal to b. These relations are known as strict inequalities. The notation a < b may also be read as 'a is strictly less than b'.

a. AD-IA Model

b. ACCRA Cost of Living Index

c. Inequality

d. ACEA agreement

9. _____s (economically referred to as land or raw materials) occur naturally within environments that exist relatively undisturbed by mankind, in a natural form. A _____'s is often characterized by amounts of biodiversity existent in various ecosystems.

Mining, petroleum extraction, fishing, hunting, and forestry are generally considered natural-resource industries.

a. 1921 recession

b. 100-year flood

c. 130-30 fund

d. Natural resource

10. In economics, a _____ exists when a specific individual or enterprise has sufficient control over a particular product or service to determine significantly the terms on which other individuals shall have access to it. Monopolies are thus characterized by a lack of economic competition for the good or service that they provide and a lack of viable substitute goods. The verb 'monopolize' refers to the process by which a firm gains persistently greater market share than what is expected under perfect competition.

a. 1921 recession   b. 130-30 fund

c. 100-year flood   d. Monopoly

11.   In economic models, the _____ time frame assumes no fixed factors of production. Firms can enter or leave the marketplace, and the cost (and availability) of land, labor, raw materials, and capital goods can be assumed to vary. In contrast, in the short-run time frame, certain factors are assumed to be fixed, because there is not sufficient time for them to change.

a. Price/performance ratio   b. Long-run

c. Diseconomies of scale   d. Productivity world

12.   This MAD scenario is often referred to as _____. The term deterrence was first used in this context after World War II; prior to that time, its use was limited to legal terminology.

In practice, the theory proved both utterly effective and exceptionally dangerous (e.g., Cuban Missile Crisis) through the end of the Cold War.

a. Sino-Soviet split   b. Nuclear deterrence

c. Berlin Wall   d. Mutual assured destruction

13.   The _____ is a Cabinet-level office, and is the largest office within the Executive Office of the President of the United States (EOP.) It is an important conduit by which the White House oversees the activities of federal agencies. OMB is tasked with giving expert advice to senior White House officials on a range of topics relating to federal policy, management, legislative, regulatory, and budgetary issues.

a. ACEA agreement   b. AD-IA Model

c. ACCRA Cost of Living Index   d. Office of Management and Budget

14.   _____ is a common concept in economics, and gives rise to derived concepts such as consumer debt. Generally _____ is defined by opposition to production. But the precise definition can vary because different schools of economists define production quite differently.

a. Foreclosure data providers   b. Federal Reserve Bank Notes

c. Cash or share options   d. Consumption

15.   _____ is an economic model based on price, utility and quantity in a market. It predicts that in a competitive market, price will function to equalize the quantity demanded by consumers, and the quantity supplied by producers, resulting in an economic equilibrium of price and quantity. The model incorporates other factors changing equilibrium as a shift of demand and/or supply.

a. Joint demand   b. Supply and demand

c. Rational addiction   d. Deferred gratification

16.   In economics, _____ is the ratio of the percent change in one variable to the percent change in another variable. It is a tool for measuring the responsiveness of a function to changes in parameters in a relative way. Commonly analyzed are _____ of substitution, price and wealth.

a. Elasticity of demand   b. ACEA agreement

c. ACCRA Cost of Living Index   d. Elasticity

17. Price _____ is defined as the measure of responsiveness in the quantity demanded for a commodity as a result of change in price of the same commodity. It is a measure of how consumers react to a change in price. In other words, it is percentage change in quantity demanded by the percentage change in price of the same commodity.
  a. ACEA agreement　　　　　　　　b. Elasticity of demand
  c. Elasticity　　　　　　　　　　　d. ACCRA Cost of Living Index

18. _____ is defined as the measure of responsiveness in the quantity demanded for a commodity as a result of change in price of the same commodity. It is a measure of how consumers react to a change in price. In other words, it is percentage change in quantity demanded as per the percentage change in price of the same commodity.
  a. Price elasticity of demand　　　　　b. 1921 recession
  c. 130-30 fund　　　　　　　　　　d. 100-year flood

19. In economics, the _____ of demand measures the responsiveness of the demand of a good to the change in the income of the people demanding the good. It is calculated as the ratio of the percent change in demand to the percent change in income. For example, if, in response to a 10% increase in income, the demand of a good increased by 20%, the _____ of demand would be 20%/10% = 2.
  a. ACEA agreement　　　　　　　　b. ACCRA Cost of Living Index
  c. AD-IA Model　　　　　　　　　　d. Income elasticity

20. In economics, the _____ measures the responsiveness of the demand of a good to the change in the income of the people demanding the good. It is calculated as the ratio of the percent change in demand to the percent change in income. For example, if, in response to a 10% increase in income, the demand of a good increased by 20%, the _____ would be 20%/10% = 2.
  a. Expenditure minimization problem　　b. Income elasticity of demand
  c. Elasticity of substitution　　　　　　d. Indifference map

21. In economics, _____ describes demand that is not very sensitive to a change in price.
  a. Export-led growth　　　　　　　　b. Inflation hedge
  c. Effective unemployment rate　　　　d. Inelastic

22. _____ is the elasticity of one variable with respect to another between two given points.

The y _____ of x is defined as:

$$E_{x,y} = \frac{\% \text{ change in } x}{\% \text{ change in } y}$$

where the percentage change is calculated relative to the midpoint

$$\% \text{ change in } x = \frac{x_2 - x_1}{(x_2 + x_1)/2}$$

$$\% \text{ change in } y = \frac{y_2 - y_1}{(y_2 + y_1)/2}$$

The midpoint _____ formula was advocated by R. G. D. Allen due to the following properties: (1) symmetric with respect to the two prices and two quantities, (2) independent of the units of measurement, and (3) yield a value of unity if the total revenues at two points are equal.

a. AD-IA Model   b. ACEA agreement
c. Arc elasticity   d. ACCRA Cost of Living Index

23.   In economics, the _____ is defined as a numerical measure of the responsiveness of the quantity supplied of product (A) to a change in price of product (A) alone. It is the measure of the way quantity supplied reacts to a change in price.

For example, if, in response to a 10% rise in the price of a good, the quantity supplied increases by 20%, the _____ would be 20%/10% = 2.

a. Passive income   b. Demand shaping
c. Hedonimetry   d. Price elasticity of supply

24.   In economics, a _____ or a hard good is a good which does not quickly wear out it yields services or utility over time rather than being completely used up when used once. Most goods are therefore _____s to a certain degree. These are goods that can last for a relatively long time, such as refrigerators, cars, and DVD players.
a. Search good   b. Superior goods
c. Luxury good   d. Durable good

25.   A _____ is an object whose consumption increases the utility of the consumer, for which the quantity demanded exceeds the quantity supplied at zero price. _____s are usually modeled as having diminishing marginal utility. The first individual purchase has high utility; the second has less.
a. Good   b. Merit good
c. Pie method   d. Composite good

26.   _____ is the observation that people often do and believe things because many other people do and believe the same things. The effect is often pejoratively called herding instinct, particularly when applied to adolescents. People tend to follow the crowd without examining the merits of a particular thing.
a. Sunk costs   b. Hyperbolic discounting
c. Halo effect   d. Bandwagon effect

27.   A _____ or complement good in economics is a good which is consumed with another good; its cross elasticity of demand is negative. - It is two goods that are bought and used together. This means that, if goods A and B were complements, more of good A being bought would result in more of good B also being bought.
a. Free good   b. Manufactured goods
c. Final good   d. Complementary Good

28.   The _____ consists of a number of economic theories which describe the nature of the firm, company including its existence, its behaviour, and its relationship with the market.

In simplified terms, the _____ aims to answer these questions:

1. Existence - why do firms emerge, why are not all transactions in the economy mediated over the market?
2. Boundaries - why the boundary between firms and the market is located exactly there? Which transactions are performed internally and which are negotiated on the market?
3. Organization - why are firms structured in such specific way? What is the interplay of formal and informal relationships?

Despite looking simple, these questions are not answered by the established economic theory, which usually views firms as given, and treats them as black boxes without any internal structure.

The First World War period saw a change of emphasis in economic theory away from industry-level analysis which mainly included analysing markets to analysis at the level of the firm, as it became increasingly clear that perfect competition was no longer an adequate model of how firms behaved. Economic theory till then had focussed on trying to understand markets alone and there had been little study on understanding why firms or organisations exist.

a. Technology gap
c. Policy Ineffectiveness Proposition

b. Theory of the firm
d. Khazzoom-Brookes postulate

29. In microeconomics, _____ is quite simply the conversion of inputs into outputs. It is an economic process that uses resources to create a good or service that is suitable for exchange. This can include manufacturing, storing, shipping, and packaging.
a. MET
c. Red Guards

b. Production
d. Solved

30. The Organization of the Petroleum Exporting Countries is a cartel of twelve countries made up of Algeria, Angola, Ecuador, Iran, Iraq, Kuwait, Libya, Nigeria, Qatar, Saudi Arabia, the United Arab Emirates, and Venezuela. The cartel has maintained its headquarters in Vienna since 1965, and hosts regular meetings among the oil ministers of its Member Countries. Indonesia withdrew its membership in _____ in 2008 after it became a net importer of oil, but stated it would likely return if it became a net exporter in the world.
a. ACEA agreement
c. OPEC

b. ACCRA Cost of Living Index
d. AD-IA Model

1. _____ is a broad label that refers to any individuals or households that use goods and services generated within the economy. The concept of a _____ is used in different contexts, so that the usage and significance of the term may vary.

Typically when business people and economists talk of _____s they are talking about person as _____, an aggregated commodity item with little individuality other than that expressed in the buy/not-buy decision.

a. 100-year flood	b. 130-30 fund
c. 1921 recession	d. Consumer

2. _____ is the study of when, why, how, where and what people do or do not buy products. It blends elements from psychology, sociology,social psychology, anthropology and economics. It attempts to understand the buyer decision making process, both individually and in groups.

a. Consumer behavior	b. Shopping Neutral
c. Consumption smoothing	d. Situational theory of publics

3. A _____ represents the combinations of goods and services that a consumer can purchase given current prices and his income. Consumer theory uses the concepts of a _____ and a preference map to analyze consumer choices. Both concepts have a ready graphical representation in the two-good case.

a. Joint demand	b. Revealed preference
c. Quality bias	d. Budget constraint

4. _____ is an online peer-reviewed magazine published by the Agricultural ' Applied Economics Association (AAEA) for readers interested in the policy and management of agriculture, the food industry, natural resources, rural communities, and the environment. _____ is published quarterly and is available free online. It is currently one of three outreach products offered by AAEA, along with the more timely Policy Issues and the forthcoming Shared Materials section of the AAEA Web site.

a. Choices	b. 1921 recession
c. 100-year flood	d. 130-30 fund

5. _____ and behavioral finance are closely related fields that have evolved to be a separate branch of economic and financial analysis which applies scientific research on human and social, cognitive and emotional factors to better understand economic decisions by consumers, borrowers, investors, and how they affect market prices, returns and the allocation of resources.

The field is primarily concerned with the bounds of rationality (selfishness, self-control) of economic agents. Behavioral models typically integrate insights from psychology with neo-classical economic theory.

a. Mainstream economics	b. Georgism
c. Neoclassical economics	d. Behavioral economics

6. The term _____ or commodity bundle refers to a fixed list of items used specifically to track the progress of inflation in an economy or specific market.

The most common type of _____ is the basket of consumer goods, used to define the Consumer Price Index (CPI.) Other types of baskets are used to define

- Producer Price Index (PPI), previously known as Wholesale Price Index (WPI)
- various commodity price indices

The term _____ analysis in the retail business refers to research that provides the retailer with information to understand the purchase behaviour of a buyer. This information will enable the retailer to understand the buyer's needs and rewrite the store's layout accordingly, develop cross-promotional programs, or even capture new buyers (much like the cross-selling concept.)

a. Category Development Index
b. Cost-weighted activity index
c. Market basket
d. Robin Hood index

7.   _____s is the social science that studies the production, distribution, and consumption of goods and services. The term _____s comes from the Ancient Greek oá¼°κονομῖα from oá¼¶κος (oikos, 'house') + vῐΌμος (nomos, 'custom' or 'law'), hence 'rules of the house(hold)'. Current _____ models developed out of the broader field of political economy in the late 19th century, owing to a desire to use an empirical approach more akin to the physical sciences.

a. Energy economics
b. Opportunity cost
c. Inflation
d. Economic

8.   In microeconomic theory, an _____ is a graph showing different bundles of goods, each measured as to quantity, between which a consumer is indifferent. That is, at each point on the curve, the consumer has no preference for one bundle over another. In other words, they are all equally preferred.

a. Indifference map
b. Indifference curve
c. Expenditure minimization problem
d. Engel curve

9.   A _____ is an object whose consumption increases the utility of the consumer, for which the quantity demanded exceeds the quantity supplied at zero price. _____s are usually modeled as having diminishing marginal utility. The first individual purchase has high utility; the second has less.

a. Composite good
b. Merit good
c. Pie method
d. Good

10.   In microeconomic theory a preference map or _____ is the collection of indifference curves possessed by an individual. Similar in nature to a topographical map, the contour lines of such a map demonstrating progressively more desirable options as they move upward or to the right. Because of the nature of indifference curves they cannot intersect and are effectively infinite in number, their sum defining all possible combinations of values.

a. Elasticity of substitution
b. Expenditure minimization problem
c. Indifference map
d. Engel curve

11.   In economics, the _____ is the rate at which a consumer is ready to give up one good in exchange for another good while maintaining the same level of satisfaction.

Under the standard assumption of neoclassical economics that goods and services are continuously divisible, the marginal rates of substitution will be the same regardless of the direction of exchange, and will correspond to the slope of an indifference curve (more precisely, to the slope multiplied by -1) passing through the consumption bundle in question, at that point: mathematically, it is the implicit derivative. MRS of Y for X is the amount of Y for which a consumer is willing to exchange for X locally.

a. Quality bias   b. Demand vacuum
c. Supply and demand   d. Marginal rate of substitution

12.   In finance, _____ is a measure of the sensitivity of the duration of a bond to changes in interest rates. There is an inverse relationship between _____ and sensitivity - in general, the higher the _____ less sensitive the bond price is to interest rate shifts, the lower the _____, the more sensitive it is.

Duration is a linear measure or 1st derivative of how the price of a bond changes in response to interest rate changes.

a. Technocracy   b. Rule
c. Russian financial crisis   d. Convexity

13.   In economics, _____ is a measure of the relative satisfaction from consumption of various goods and services. Given this measure, one may speak meaningfully of increasing or decreasing _____, and thereby explain economic behavior in terms of attempts to increase one's _____. For illustrative purposes, changes in _____ are sometimes expressed in units called utils.

a. Ordinal utility   b. Expected utility hypothesis
c. Utility   d. Utility function

14.   In economics, the _____ functional form of production functions is widely used to represent the relationship of an output to inputs. It was proposed by Knut Wicksell (1851-1926), and tested against statistical evidence by Charles Cobb and Paul Douglas in 1900-1928.

For production, the function is

$$Y = AL^{\alpha}K^{\beta},$$

where:

- Y = total production (the monetary value of all goods produced in a year)
- L = labor input
- K = capital input
- A = total factor productivity
- α and β are the output elasticities of labor and capital, respectively. These values are constants determined by available technology.

Output elasticity measures the responsiveness of output to a change in levels of either labor or capital used in production, ceteris paribus. For example if α = 0.15, a 1% increase in labor would lead to approximately a 0.15% increase in output.

a. Demand-pull theory

b. Growth accounting

c. Social savings

d. Cobb-Douglas

15. While preferences are the conventional foundation of microeconomics, it is often convenient to represent preferences with a _____ and reason indirectly about preferences with _____s. Let X be the consumption set, the set of all mutually-exclusive packages the consumer could conceivably consume (such as an indifference curve map without the indifference curves.) The consumer's _____ $u : X \rightarrow \mathbf{R}$ ranks each package in the consumption set.

a. Utility

b. Expected utility hypothesis

c. Ordinal utility

d. Utility function

16. In economics, _____ is a theory of utility under which the utility (roughly, satisfaction) gained from a particular good or service can be measured and that the magnitude of the measurement is meaningful. Under _____ theory, the util is a unit of measurement much like the metre or second. A util has a fixed size, making comparisons based on ratios of utils possible.

a. Cardinal utility

b. 130-30 fund

c. Weakly additive

d. 100-year flood

17. _____ theory states that while the utility of a particular good and service cannot be measured using an objective scale, a consumer is capable of ranking different alternatives available. Goods are often considered in 'bundles' or 'baskets'. For example, does individual A prefer 3 apples and 2 oranges or 3 oranges and 2 apples? When a large number of baskets of goods are compared, the preferences of the individual can be seen.

a. Utility function

b. Expected utility hypothesis

c. Utility

d. Ordinal utility

18. _____ in economics and business is the result of an exchange and from that trade we assign a numerical monetary value to a good, service or asset. If Alice trades Bob 4 apples for an orange, the _____ of an orange is 4 apples. Inversely, the _____ of an apple is 1/4 oranges.

a. Premium pricing

b. Price book

c. Price

d. Price war

19. _____ refers to a business or organization attempting to acquire goods or services to accomplish the goals of the enterprise. Though there are several organizations that attempt to set standards in the _____ process, processes can vary greatly between organizations. Typically the word '_____' is not used interchangeably with the word 'procurement', since procurement typically includes Expediting, Supplier Quality, and Traffic and Logistics (T'L) in addition to _____.

a. Free port

b. 130-30 fund

c. 100-year flood

d. Purchasing

20. _____ is the number of goods/services that can be purchased with a unit of currency. For example, if you had taken one dollar to a store in the 1950s, you would have been able to buy a greater number of items than you would today, indicating that you would have had a greater _____ in the 1950s. Currency can be either a commodity money, like gold or silver, or fiat currency like US dollars.

a. Purchasing power   b. Human Poverty Index

c. Compliance cost   d. Genuine progress indicator

21.   In economics and finance, _____ is the change in total cost that arises when the quantity produced changes by one unit. It is the cost of producing one more unit of a good. Mathematically, the _____ function is expressed as the first derivative of the total cost (TC) function with respect to quantity (Q.)

a. Marginal cost   b. Variable cost

c. Khozraschyot   d. Quality costs

22.   A _____ is a special solution to an agent's maximization problem in which the quantity of one of the arguments in the maximized function is zero. The more usual solution will lie in the non-zero interior at the point of tangency between the objective function and the constraint. For example, in consumer theory the objective function is the indifference-curve map (the utility function) of the consumer.

a. Corner solution   b. 100-year flood

c. 1921 recession   d. 130-30 fund

23.   _____ theory, pioneered by American economist Paul Samuelson, is a method by which it is possible to discern the best possible option on the basis of consumer behavior. Essentially, this means that the preferences of consumers can be revealed by their purchasing habits. _____ theory came about because the theories of consumer demand were based on a diminishing marginal rate of substitution (MRS.)

a. Joint demand   b. Rational addiction

c. Marginal rate of substitution   d. Revealed preference

24.   In economics, the _____ of a good or of a service is the utility of the specific use to which an agent would put a given increase in that good or service, or of the specific use that would be abandoned in response to a given decrease. In other words, _____ is the utility of the marginal use -- which, on the assumption of economic rationality, would be the least urgent use of the good or service, from the best feasible combination of actions in which its use is included. Under the mainstream assumptions, the _____ of a good or service is the posited quantified change in utility obtained by increasing or by decreasing use of that good or service.

a. Marginal utility   b. 1921 recession

c. 100-year flood   d. 130-30 fund

25.   Economics:

- _____,the desire to own something and the ability to pay for it
- _____ curve,a graphic representation of a _____ schedule
- _____ deposit, the money in checking accounts
- _____ pull theory,the theory that inflation occurs when _____ for goods and services exceeds existing supplies
- _____ schedule,a table that lists the quantity of a good a person will buy it each different price
- _____ side economics,the school of economics at believes government spending and tax cuts open economy by raising _____

a. Demand

b. McKesson ' Robbins scandal

c. Variability

d. Production

26. _____ is the controlled distribution of resources and scarce goods or services. _____ controls the size of the ration, one's allotted portion of the resources being distributed on a particular day or at a particular time.

In economics, it is often common to use the word '_____' to refer to one of the roles that prices play in markets, while _____ is called 'non-price _____.' Using prices to ration means that those with the most money (or other assets) and who want a product the most are first to receive it.

a. Rationing

b. 100-year flood

c. 1921 recession

d. 130-30 fund

27. A _____ is a measure of the average price of consumer goods and services purchased by households. A _____ measures a price change for a constant market basket of goods and services from one period to the next within the same area (city, region, or nation.) It is a price index determined by measuring the price of a standard group of goods meant to represent the typical market basket of a typical urban consumer.

a. Lipstick index

b. Consumer Price Index

c. Cost-of-living index

d. CPI

28. A _____ is a theoretical price index that measures relative cost of living over time. It is an index that measures differences in the price of goods and services, and allows for substitutions to other items as prices change.

There are many different methodologies that have been developed to approximate _____es, including methods that allow for substitution among items as relative prices change.

a. Lipstick index

b. CPI

c. Hedonic price index

d. Cost-of-living index

29. A _____ is a normalized average (typically a weighted average) of prices for a given class of goods or services in a given region, during a given interval of time. It is a statistic designed to help to compare how these prices, taken as a whole, differ between time periods or geographical locations.

Price indices have several potential uses.

a. Transactional Net Margin Method

b. Two-part tariff

c. Product sabotage

d. Price Index

30. _____ is a term used to described a tendency or preference towards a particular perspective, ideology or result, especially when the tendency interferes with the ability to be impartial, unprejudiced, or objective. The term _____ed is used to describe an action, judgment, or other outcome influenced by a prejudged perspective. It is also used to refer to a person or body of people whose actions or judgments exhibit _____.

a. 130-30 fund

b. 100-year flood

c. 1921 recession

d. Bias

31.   A consumer price index (_____) is a measure of the average price of consumer goods and services purchased by households. A consumer price index measures a price change for a constant market basket of goods and services from one period to the next within the same area (city, region, or nation.) It is a price index determined by measuring the price of a standard group of goods meant to represent the typical market basket of a typical urban consumer.

a. Hedonic price index   b. Cost-of-living index

c. Lipstick index   d. CPI

1. Economics:

    *   _____,the desire to own something and the ability to pay for it
    *   _____ curve,a graphic representation of a _____ schedule
    *   _____ deposit, the money in checking accounts
    *   _____ pull theory,the theory that inflation occurs when _____ for goods and services exceeds existing supplies
    *   _____ schedule,a table that lists the quantity of a good a person will buy it each different price
    *   _____ side economics,the school of economics at believes government spending and tax cuts open economy by raising _____

    a. Production

    b. McKesson ' Robbins scandal

    c. Demand

    d. Variability

2. In economics, the _____ can be defined as the graph depicting the relationship between the price of a certain commodity, and the amount of it that consumers are willing and able to purchase at that given price. It is a graphic representation of a demand schedule. The _____ for all consumers together follows from the _____ of every individual consumer: the individual demands at each price are added together.

    a. Kuznets curve

    b. Wage curve

    c. Cost curve

    d. Demand curve

3. _____ is the observation that people often do and believe things because many other people do and believe the same things. The effect is often pejoratively called herding instinct, particularly when applied to adolescents. People tend to follow the crowd without examining the merits of a particular thing.

    a. Sunk costs

    b. Halo effect

    c. Hyperbolic discounting

    d. Bandwagon effect

4. In economics, the _____ is the rate at which a consumer is ready to give up one good in exchange for another good while maintaining the same level of satisfaction.

    Under the standard assumption of neoclassical economics that goods and services are continuously divisible, the marginal rates of substitution will be the same regardless of the direction of exchange, and will correspond to the slope of an indifference curve (more precisely, to the slope multiplied by -1) passing through the consumption bundle in question, at that point: mathematically, it is the implicit derivative. MRS of Y for X is the amount of Y for which a consumer is willing to exchange for X locally.

    a. Quality bias

    b. Supply and demand

    c. Demand vacuum

    d. Marginal rate of substitution

5. In economics, _____ is the ratio of the percent change in one variable to the percent change in another variable. It is a tool for measuring the responsiveness of a function to changes in parameters in a relative way. Commonly analyzed are _____ of substitution, price and wealth.

    a. Elasticity

    b. Elasticity of demand

    c. ACEA agreement

    d. ACCRA Cost of Living Index

6.   Price _____ is defined as the measure of responsiveness in the quantity demanded for a commodity as a result of change in price of the same commodity. It is a measure of how consumers react to a change in price. In other words, it is percentage change in quantity demanded by the percentage change in price of the same commodity.
   a. Elasticity   b. ACEA agreement
   c. ACCRA Cost of Living Index   d. Elasticity of demand

7.   In economics, an _____ shows how the quantity demanded of a good or service changes as the consumer's income level changes. It is named after the 19th century German statistician Ernst Engel.

Graphically, the _____ is represented in the first-quadrant of the cartesian coordinate system.

   a. Induced consumption   b. Utility maximization problem
   c. Expenditure minimization problem   d. Engel curve

8.   In economics, the _____ of demand measures the responsiveness of the demand of a good to the change in the income of the people demanding the good. It is calculated as the ratio of the percent change in demand to the percent change in income. For example, if, in response to a 10% increase in income, the demand of a good increased by 20%, the _____ of demand would be 20%/10% = 2.
   a. ACEA agreement   b. ACCRA Cost of Living Index
   c. AD-IA Model   d. Income elasticity

9.   In economics, the _____ measures the responsiveness of the demand of a good to the change in the income of the people demanding the good. It is calculated as the ratio of the percent change in demand to the percent change in income. For example, if, in response to a 10% increase in income, the demand of a good increased by 20%, the _____ would be 20%/10% = 2.
   a. Elasticity of substitution   b. Expenditure minimization problem
   c. Indifference map   d. Income elasticity of demand

10.   In consumer theory, an _____ is a good that decreases in demand when consumer income rises, unlike normal goods, for which the opposite is observed. It is a good that consumers demand increases when their income increases. Inferiority, in this sense, is an observable fact relating to affordability rather than a statement about the quality of the good.
   a. Independent goods   b. Inferior good
   c. Information good   d. Export-oriented

11.   In economics, _____s are any goods for which demand increases when income increases and falls when income decreases but price remains constant, i.e. with a positive income elasticity of demand. The term does not necessarily refer to the quality of the good.

Depending on the indifference curves, the amount of a good bought can either increase, decrease, or stay the same when income increases.

   a. Normative economics   b. Bord halfpenny
   c. Financial contagion   d. Normal good

12. A _____ is an object whose consumption increases the utility of the consumer, for which the quantity demanded exceeds the quantity supplied at zero price. _____s are usually modeled as having diminishing marginal utility. The first individual purchase has high utility; the second has less.

   a. Merit good   b. Composite good

   c. Pie method   d. Good

13. _____ is a broad label that refers to any individuals or households that use goods and services generated within the economy. The concept of a _____ is used in different contexts, so that the usage and significance of the term may vary.

Typically when business people and economists talk of _____s they are talking about person as _____, an aggregated commodity item with little individuality other than that expressed in the buy/not-buy decision.

   a. Consumer   b. 130-30 fund

   c. 1921 recession   d. 100-year flood

14. _____ is the study of when, why, how, where and what people do or do not buy products. It blends elements from psychology, sociology,social psychology, anthropology and economics. It attempts to understand the buyer decision making process, both individually and in groups.

   a. Consumption smoothing   b. Shopping Neutral

   c. Situational theory of publics   d. Consumer behavior

15. In economics, the _____ is the change in consumption resulting from a change in real income.

Another important item that can change is the money income of the consumer. The _____ is the phenomenon observed through changes in purchasing power.

   a. Export subsidy   b. Inflation hedge

   c. Equilibrium wage   d. Income effect

16. In economics and consumer theory, a _____ is one which people consume more of as price rises, violating the law of demand. In normal situations, as the price of such a good rises, the substitution effect causes people to purchase less of it and more of substitute goods. In the _____ situation, cheaper close substitutes are not available.

   a. Search good   b. Giffen good

   c. Pie method   d. Demerit good

17. To _____ is to impose a financial charge or other levy upon a taxpayer by a state or the functional equivalent of a state.

_____es are also imposed by many subnational entities. _____es consist of direct _____ or indirect _____, and may be paid in money or as its labour equivalent (often but not always unpaid.)

   a. 1921 recession   b. 130-30 fund

   c. 100-year flood   d. Tax

18. A _____ is a price discrimination technique in which the price of a product or service is composed of two parts - a lump-sum fee as well as a per-unit charge. In general, price discrimination techniques only occur in partially or fully monopolistic markets. It is designed to enable the firm to capture more consumer surplus than it otherwise would in a non-discriminating pricing environment.

a. Price floor

b. Big ticket item

c. Penetration pricing

d. Two-part tariff

19. A _____ is a duty imposed on goods when they are moved across a political boundary. They are usually associated with protectionism, the economic policy of restraining trade between nations. For political reasons, _____s are usually imposed on imported goods, although they may also be imposed on exported goods.

a. 100-year flood

b. 1921 recession

c. 130-30 fund

d. Tariff

20. The term surplus is used in economics for several related quantities. The _____ is the amount that consumers benefit by being able to purchase a product for a price that is less than they would be willing to pay. The producer surplus is the amount that producers benefit by selling at a market price mechanism that is higher than they would be willing to sell for.

a. Consumer surplus

b. Necessity good

c. Microeconomic reform

d. Marginal rate of technical substitution

21. _____ in economics and business is the result of an exchange and from that trade we assign a numerical monetary value to a good, service or asset. If Alice trades Bob 4 apples for an orange, the _____ of an orange is 4 apples. Inversely, the _____ of an apple is 1/4 oranges.

a. Premium pricing

b. Price war

c. Price book

d. Price

22. _____ is defined as the measure of responsiveness in the quantity demanded for a commodity as a result of change in price of the same commodity. It is a measure of how consumers react to a change in price. In other words, it is percentage change in quantity demanded as per the percentage change in price of the same commodity.

a. 1921 recession

b. 100-year flood

c. 130-30 fund

d. Price elasticity of demand

23. In economics, _____ describes demand that is not very sensitive to a change in price.

a. Export-led growth

b. Effective unemployment rate

c. Inflation hedge

d. Inelastic

24. In economics, _____ is the total demand for final goods and services in the economy (Y) at a given time and price level. It is the amount of goods and services in the economy that will be purchased at all possible price levels. This is the demand for the gross domestic product of a country when inventory levels are static.

a. Aggregate demand

b. Aggregation problem

c. Aggregate supply

d. Aggregate expenditure

25. The _____ refers to the desire to own exclusive or unique goods. These goods usually have a high economic value, but low practical value. The less of an item available, the higher its snob value.

a. Demand vacuum

b. Deferred gratification

c. Snob effect

d. Cross elasticity of demand

26.   The _____ consists of a number of economic theories which describe the nature of the firm, company including its existence, its behaviour, and its relationship with the market.

In simplified terms, the _____ aims to answer these questions:

1.   Existence - why do firms emerge, why are not all transactions in the economy mediated over the market?
2.   Boundaries - why the boundary between firms and the market is located exactly there? Which transactions are performed internally and which are negotiated on the market?
3.   Organization - why are firms structured in such specific way? What is the interplay of formal and informal relationships?

Despite looking simple, these questions are not answered by the established economic theory, which usually views firms as given, and treats them as black boxes without any internal structure.

The First World War period saw a change of emphasis in economic theory away from industry-level analysis which mainly included analysing markets to analysis at the level of the firm, as it became increasingly clear that perfect competition was no longer an adequate model of how firms behaved. Economic theory till then had focussed on trying to understand markets alone and there had been little study on understanding why firms or organisations exist.

a. Theory of the firm
c. Khazzoom-Brookes postulate

b. Technology gap
d. Policy Ineffectiveness Proposition

27.   In economics, the _____ functional form of production functions is widely used to represent the relationship of an output to inputs. It was proposed by Knut Wicksell (1851-1926), and tested against statistical evidence by Charles Cobb and Paul Douglas in 1900-1928.

For production, the function is

$$Y = AL^{\alpha}K^{\beta},$$

where:

- Y = total production (the monetary value of all goods produced in a year)
- L = labor input
- K = capital input
- A = total factor productivity
- α and β are the output elasticities of labor and capital, respectively. These values are constants determined by available technology.

Output elasticity measures the responsiveness of output to a change in levels of either labor or capital used in production, ceteris paribus. For example if α = 0.15, a 1% increase in labor would lead to approximately a 0.15% increase in output.

a. Social savings
c. Cobb-Douglas

b. Growth accounting
d. Demand-pull theory

28.   In economics, the _____ of a good or of a service is the utility of the specific use to which an agent would put a given increase in that good or service, or of the specific use that would be abandoned in response to a given decrease. In other words, _____ is the utility of the marginal use -- which, on the assumption of economic rationality, would be the least urgent use of the good or service, from the best feasible combination of actions in which its use is included. Under the mainstream assumptions, the _____ of a good or service is the posited quantified change in utility obtained by increasing or by decreasing use of that good or service.

a. 100-year flood
c. 1921 recession

b. 130-30 fund
d. Marginal utility

29.   In economics, _____ is a measure of the relative satisfaction from consumption of various goods and services. Given this measure, one may speak meaningfully of increasing or decreasing _____, and thereby explain economic behavior in terms of attempts to increase one's _____. For illustrative purposes, changes in _____ are sometimes expressed in units called utils.

a. Ordinal utility
c. Expected utility hypothesis

b. Utility function
d. Utility

30.   A _____ is one scenario provided for evaluation by respondents in a Choice Experiment. Responses are collected and used to create a Choice Model. Respondents are usually provided with a series of differing _____s for evaluation.

a. 100-year flood
c. 1921 recession

b. Choice Set
d. 130-30 fund

31.   In mathematical optimization, the method of _____s provides a strategy for finding the maximum/minimum of a function subject to constraints.

For example , consider the optimization problem

maximize $f(x, y)$
subject to $g(x, y) = c.$

We introduce a new variable (λ) called a _____, and study the Lagrange function defined by

$$\Lambda(x, y, \lambda) = f(x, y) + \lambda\Big(g(x, y) - c\Big).$$

(λ may be either added or subtracted.) If (x,y)‰ is a maximum for the original constrained problem, then there exists a λ such that (x,y,λ)‰ is a stationary point for the Lagrange function (stationary points are those points where the partial derivatives of Λ are zero.)

a. Lagrange multiplier
c. 130-30 fund

b. Radfar ratio
d. 100-year flood

32. While preferences are the conventional foundation of microeconomics, it is often convenient to represent preferences with a _____ and reason indirectly about preferences with _____s. Let X be the consumption set, the set of all mutually-exclusive packages the consumer could conceivably consume (such as an indifference curve map without the indifference curves.) The consumer's _____ $u : X \longrightarrow \mathbf{R}$ ranks each package in the consumption set.
  a. Utility
  b. Utility function
  c. Expected utility hypothesis
  d. Ordinal utility

33. _____ is a theory of microeconomics that relates preferences to consumer demand curves. The link between personal preferences, consumption, and the demand curve is one of the most complex relations in economics. Implicitly, economists assume that anything purchased will be consumed, unless the purchase is for a productive activity.
  a. Rational choice theory
  b. Literacy rate
  c. Consumer theory
  d. Financial crisis

34. The _____ in economics relates changes in Marshallian demand to changes in Hicksian demand. It demonstrates that demand changes due to price changes are a result of two effects:

  - a substitution effect, the result of a change in the exchange rate between two goods; and
  - an income effect, the effect of price results in a change of the consumer's purchasing power.

Each element of the Slutsky matrix is given by

$$\frac{\partial x_i(p,w)}{\partial p_j} = \frac{\partial h_i(p,u)}{\partial p_j} - \frac{\partial x_i(p,w)}{\partial w}x_j(p,w),$$

where h(p,u) is the Hicksian demand and x(p,w) is the Marshallian demand, at price level p, wealth level w, and utility level u. The first term represents the substitution effect, and the second term represents the income effect.

The same equation can be rewritten in matrix form and is called the Slutsky matrix

$$D_p x(p,w) = D_p h(p,u) - D_w x(p,w)x(p,w)^\top,$$

where D_p is the derivative operator with respect to price and D_w is the derivative operator with respect to wealth.

  a. 130-30 fund
  b. Slutsky equation
  c. Simultaneous equations
  d. 100-year flood

1. _____ is a broad label that refers to any individuals or households that use goods and services generated within the economy. The concept of a _____ is used in different contexts, so that the usage and significance of the term may vary.

Typically when business people and economists talk of _____s they are talking about person as _____, an aggregated commodity item with little individuality other than that expressed in the buy/not-buy decision.

   a. 100-year flood   b. 130-30 fund
   c. 1921 recession   d. Consumer

2. _____ is the study of when, why, how, where and what people do or do not buy products. It blends elements from psychology, sociology,social psychology, anthropology and economics. It attempts to understand the buyer decision making process, both individually and in groups.

   a. Consumer behavior   b. Shopping Neutral
   c. Consumption smoothing   d. Situational theory of publics

3. _____ is a way of expressing knowledge or belief that an event will occur or has occurred. In mathematics the concept has been given an exact meaning in _____ theory, that is used extensively in such areas of study as mathematics, statistics, finance, gambling, science, and philosophy to draw conclusions about the likelihood of potential events and the underlying mechanics of complex systems.

The word _____ does not have a consistent direct definition.

   a. 1921 recession   b. 130-30 fund
   c. 100-year flood   d. Probability

4. In probability theory and statistics, the _____ (or expectation value or mean and for continuous random variables with a density function it is the probability density -weighted integral of the possible values.

The term '_____' can be misleading.

   a. AD-IA Model   b. ACCRA Cost of Living Index
   c. Expected value   d. ACEA agreement

5. The term _____, 'the state or characteristic of being variable',_____ describes how spread out or closely clustered a set of data is. may be applied to many different subjects:

- Climate _____
- Genetic _____
- Heart rate _____
- Human _____
- Solar van
- Spatial _____
- Statistical _____
- _____

.

a. Characteristic	b. Total product
c. Demand	d. Variability

6. _____ is the a method of technical and economic research of the systems for purpose to optimize a parity between system's consumer functions or properties and expenses to achieve those functions or properties.

This methodology for continuous perfection of production, industrial technologies, organizational structures was developed by Juryj Sobolev in 1948 at the 'Perm telephone factory'

- 1948 Juryj Sobolev - the first success in application of a method analysis at the 'Perm telephone factory' .
- 1949 - the first application for the invention as result of use of the new method.

Today in economically developed countries practically each enterprise or the company use methodology of the kind of functional-cost analysis as a practice of the quality management, most full satisfying to principles of standards of series ISO 9000.

- Interest of consumer not in products itself, but the advantage which it will receive from its usage.
- The consumer aspires to reduce his expenses
- Functions needed by consumer can be executed in the various ways, and, hence, with various efficiency and expenses. Among possible alternatives of realization of functions exist such in which the parity of quality and the price is the optimal for the consumer.

The goal of _____ is achievement of the highest consumer satisfaction of production at simultaneous decrease in all kinds of industrial expenses Classical _____ has three English synonyms - Value Engineering, Value Management, Value Analysis.

a. Staple financing	b. Willingness to pay
c. Monopoly wage	d. Function cost analysis

7. In probability theory and statistics, _____ is a measure of the variability or dispersion of a population, a data set, or a probability distribution. A low _____ indicates that the data points tend to be very close to the same value (the mean), while high _____ indicates that the data are 'spread out' over a large range of values.

For example, the average height for adult men in the United States is about 70 inches, with a _____ of around 3 inches.

a. 100-year flood   b. 130-30 fund
c. Standard deviation   d. 1921 recession

8.   In economics, the _____ functional form of production functions is widely used to represent the relationship of an output to inputs. It was proposed by Knut Wicksell (1851-1926), and tested against statistical evidence by Charles Cobb and Paul Douglas in 1900-1928.

For production, the function is

$$Y = AL^{\alpha}K^{\beta},$$

where:

- Y = total production (the monetary value of all goods produced in a year)
- L = labor input
- K = capital input
- A = total factor productivity
- α and β are the output elasticities of labor and capital, respectively. These values are constants determined by available technology.

Output elasticity measures the responsiveness of output to a change in levels of either labor or capital used in production, ceteris paribus. For example if $\alpha = 0.15$, a 1% increase in labor would lead to approximately a 0.15% increase in output.

a. Growth accounting   b. Social savings
c. Demand-pull theory   d. Cobb-Douglas

9.   In economics, game theory, and decision theory the _____ theorem or _____ hypothesis predicts that the 'betting preferences' of people with regard to uncertain outcomes (gambles) can be described by a mathematical relation which takes into account the size of a payout (whether in money or other goods), the probability of occurrence, risk aversion, and the different utility of the same payout to people with different assets or personal preferences. It is a more sophisticated theory than simply predicting that choices will be made based on expected value (which takes into account only the size of the payout and the probability of occurrence.)

Daniel Bernoulli described the complete theory in 1738.

a. Utility   b. Expected utility hypothesis
c. Ordinal utility   d. Expected utility

10.   In economics, the _____ of a good or of a service is the utility of the specific use to which an agent would put a given increase in that good or service, or of the specific use that would be abandoned in response to a given decrease. In other words, _____ is the utility of the marginal use -- which, on the assumption of economic rationality, would be the least urgent use of the good or service, from the best feasible combination of actions in which its use is included. Under the mainstream assumptions, the _____ of a good or service is the posited quantified change in utility obtained by increasing or by decreasing use of that good or service.

   a. 1921 recession
   c. Marginal utility

   b. 130-30 fund
   d. 100-year flood

11.   In economics, _____ is a measure of the relative satisfaction from consumption of various goods and services. Given this measure, one may speak meaningfully of increasing or decreasing _____, and thereby explain economic behavior in terms of attempts to increase one's _____. For illustrative purposes, changes in _____ are sometimes expressed in units called utils.

   a. Expected utility hypothesis
   c. Utility

   b. Utility function
   d. Ordinal utility

12.   _____ is a concept in economics, finance, and psychology related to the behaviour of consumers and investors under uncertainty. _____ is the reluctance of a person to accept a bargain with an uncertain payoff rather than another bargain with a more certain, but possibly lower, expected payoff. For example, a risk-averse investor might choose to put his or her money into a bank account with a low but guaranteed interest rate, rather than into a stock that is likely to have high returns, but also has a chance of becoming worthless.

   a. Risk aversion
   c. Reinsurance

   b. Compound annual growth rate
   d. Risk theory

13.   In economics, _____ behavior is in between risk aversion and risk seeking. If offered either â¬50 or a 50% chance of â¬100, a risk averse person will take the â¬50, a risk seeking person will take the 50% chance of â¬100, and a _____ person would have no preference between the two options.

In finance, when pricing an asset, a common technique is to figure out the probability of a future cash flow, then to discount that cash flow at the risk free rate.

   a. Risk neutral
   c. Transaction risk

   b. Currency risk
   d. Taleb distribution

14.   A _____ is the minimum difference a person requires to be willing to take an uncertain bet, between the expected value of the bet and the certain value that he is indifferent to.

The certainty equivalent is the guaranteed payoff at which a person is 'indifferent' between accepting the guaranteed payoff and a higher but uncertain payoff. (It is the amount of the higher payout minus the _____.)

   a. Linear model
   c. Ruin theory

   b. Workers compensation
   d. Risk premium

15.   In microeconomic theory, an _____ is a graph showing different bundles of goods, each measured as to quantity, between which a consumer is indifferent. That is, at each point on the curve, the consumer has no preference for one bundle over another. In other words, they are all equally preferred.
a. Indifference curve
b. Indifference map
c. Expenditure minimization problem
d. Engel curve

16.   A _____ is a professionally managed type of collective investment scheme that pools money from many investors and invests it in stocks, bonds, short-term money market instruments, and/or other securities. The _____ will have a fund manager that trades the pooled money on a regular basis. As of early 2008, the worldwide value of all _____s totals more than $26 trillion.
a. Dark pools of liquidity
b. Participating policy
c. Self-invested personal pension
d. Mutual fund

17.   _____ is the revenue to a brokerage firm when commissioned securities and insurance salespeople sell a product, whether it is an investment like stocks, bonds or insurance like life insurance or long term care insurance. The commission that the agent receives is usually a percentage of this figure, although some firms like Merrill Lynch use figures called Production Credits, usually smaller than _____, to determine payouts and retain more revenue.

For example, a mutual fund with a 5.75% sales charge is sold to someone who invests $10,000.

a. Gross Dealer Concession
b. Monopoly price
c. Discretionary policy
d. Number of Shares

18.   A _____ is a public market for the trading of company stock and derivatives at an agreed price; these are securities listed on a stock exchange as well as those only traded privately.

The size of the world _____ was estimated at about $36.6 trillion US at the beginning of October 2008 . The total world derivatives market has been estimated at about $791 trillion face or nominal value, 11 times the size of the entire world economy.

a. Adam Smith
b. Adolph Fischer
c. Adolf Hitler
d. Stock market

19.   In economics, _____ is the active redirecting resources from being consumed today so that they may create benefits in the future; the use of assets to earn income or profit._____ is the process of making an investment in order to earn a profit, for example equity investment either through a fund, a 401k plan, or individually. People often invest in order to build up their estate or to accumulate funds for retirement.

To try to predict good stocks to invest in, two main schools of thought exist: technical analysis and fundamentals analysis.

a. AD-IA Model
b. ACEA agreement
c. ACCRA Cost of Living Index
d. Investing

20. _____, in law and economics, is a form of risk management primarily used to hedge against the risk of a contingent loss. _____ is defined as the equitable transfer of the risk of a loss, from one entity to another, in exchange for a premium, and can be thought of as a guaranteed small loss to prevent a large, possibly devastating loss. An insurer is a company selling the _____; an insured or policyholder is the person or entity buying the _____.

a. AD-IA Model

c. Insurance

b. ACEA agreement

d. ACCRA Cost of Living Index

21. _____ describes a deliberate attempt to interfere with the free and fair operation of the market and create artificial, false or misleading appearances with respect to the price of a security, commodity or currency. _____ is prohibited under Section 9(a)(2) of the Securities Exchange Act of 1934, and in Australia under Section s 1041A of the Corporations Act 2001. The Act defines _____ as transactions which create an artificial price or maintain an artificial price for a tradable security.

a. Net domestic product

c. Managerial economics

b. Market manipulation

d. Legal monopoly

22. Economics:

- _____,the desire to own something and the ability to pay for it
- _____ curve,a graphic representation of a _____ schedule
- _____ deposit, the money in checking accounts
- _____ pull theory,the theory that inflation occurs when _____ for goods and services exceeds existing supplies
- _____ schedule,a table that lists the quantity of a good a person will buy it each different price
- _____ side economics,the school of economics at believes government spending and tax cuts open economy by raising _____

a. Production

c. Variability

b. Demand

d. McKesson ' Robbins scandal

23. _____ is a term used in economics and game theory to describe an economic situation or game in which knowledge about other market participants or players is available to all participants. Every player knows the payoffs and strategies available to other players.

_____ is one of the theoretical pre-conditions of an efficient perfectly competitive market.

a. Metagame analysis

c. Repeated game

b. Replicator equation

d. Complete information

24. In business and accounting, _____ are everything of value that is owned by a person or company. It is a claim on the property your income of a borrower. The balance sheet of a firm records the monetary value of the _____ owned by the firm.

a. ACEA agreement

c. ACCRA Cost of Living Index

b. Amortization schedule

d. Assets

25. The _____ is the weighted-average most likely outcome in gambling, probability theory, economics or finance.

What Does _____ Mean? The average of a probability distribution of possible returns, calculated by using the following formula:

E(R)= Sum: probability (in scenario i) * the return (in scenario i)

How do you calculate the average of a probability distribution? As denoted by the above formula, simply take the probability of each possible return outcome and multiply it by the return outcome itself. For example, if you knew a given investment had a 50% chance of earning a 10% return, a 25% chance of earning 20% and a 25% chance of earning -10%, the _____ would be equal to 7.5%:

= (0.5) (0.1) + (0.25) (0.2) + (0.25) (-0.1) = 0.075 = 7.5%

Although this is what you expect the return to be, there is no guarantee that it will be the actual return.

a. ACEA agreement   b. AD-IA Model
c. ACCRA Cost of Living Index   d. Expected return

26. In finance, _____ rate of profit or sometimes just return, is the ratio of money gained or lost on an investment relative to the amount of money invested. The amount of money gained or lost may be referred to as interest, profit/loss, gain/loss, or net income/loss. The money invested may be referred to as the asset, capital, principal, or the cost basis of the investment.
a. Current ratio   b. Sortino ratio
c. Cost accrual ratio   d. Rate of Return

27. A _____ is a situation that involves losing one quality or aspect of something in return for gaining another quality or aspect. It implies a decision to be made with full comprehension of both the upside and downside of a particular choice.

In economics the term is expressed as opportunity cost, referring the most preferred alternative given up.

a. Friedman-Savage utility function   b. Whitemail
c. Nonmarket   d. Trade-off

28. _____ in economics and business is the result of an exchange and from that trade we assign a numerical monetary value to a good, service or asset. If Alice trades Bob 4 apples for an orange, the _____ of an orange is 4 apples. Inversely, the _____ of an apple is 1/4 oranges.
a. Price   b. Price book
c. Premium pricing   d. Price war

29. _____ and behavioral finance are closely related fields that have evolved to be a separate branch of economic and financial analysis which applies scientific research on human and social, cognitive and emotional factors to better understand economic decisions by consumers, borrowers, investors, and how they affect market prices, returns and the allocation of resources.

The field is primarily concerned with the bounds of rationality (selfishness, self-control) of economic agents. Behavioral models typically integrate insights from psychology with neo-classical economic theory.

a. Neoclassical economics

b. Behavioral economics

c. Georgism

d. Mainstream economics

30. _____s is the social science that studies the production, distribution, and consumption of goods and services. The term _____s comes from the Ancient Greek oá¼°κονομῖα from oá¼¶κος (oikos, 'house') + vÏŒμος (nomos, 'custom' or 'law'), hence 'rules of the house(hold)'. Current _____ models developed out of the broader field of political economy in the late 19th century, owing to a desire to use an empirical approach more akin to the physical sciences.

a. Inflation

b. Economic

c. Opportunity cost

d. Energy economics

31. _____ is the term denoting either an entrance or changes which are inserted into a system and which activate/modify a process. It is an abstract concept, used in the modeling, system(s) design and system(s) exploitation. It is usually connected with other terms, e.g., _____ field, _____ variable, _____ parameter, _____ value, _____ signal, _____ device and _____ file.

a. ACEA agreement

b. ACCRA Cost of Living Index

c. AD-IA Model

d. Input

1. The _____ consists of a number of economic theories which describe the nature of the firm, company including its existence, its behaviour, and its relationship with the market.

In simplified terms, the _____ aims to answer these questions:

1. Existence - why do firms emerge, why are not all transactions in the economy mediated over the market?
2. Boundaries - why the boundary between firms and the market is located exactly there? Which transactions are performed internally and which are negotiated on the market?
3. Organization - why are firms structured in such specific way? What is the interplay of formal and informal relationships?

Despite looking simple, these questions are not answered by the established economic theory, which usually views firms as given, and treats them as black boxes without any internal structure.

The First World War period saw a change of emphasis in economic theory away from industry-level analysis which mainly included analysing markets to analysis at the level of the firm, as it became increasingly clear that perfect competition was no longer an adequate model of how firms behaved. Economic theory till then had focussed on trying to understand markets alone and there had been little study on understanding why firms or organisations exist.

a. Policy Ineffectiveness Proposition   b. Theory of the firm
c. Technology gap   d. Khazzoom-Brookes postulate

2. In microeconomics, _____ is quite simply the conversion of inputs into outputs. It is an economic process that uses resources to create a good or service that is suitable for exchange. This can include manufacturing, storing, shipping, and packaging.
    a. Red Guards   b. Production
    c. MET   d. Solved

3. In economics, _____ are the resources employed to produce goods and services. They facilitate production but do not become part of the product (as with raw materials) or significantly transformed by the production process (as with fuel used to power machinery.) To 19th century economists, the _____ were land (natural resources, gifts from nature), labor (the ability to work), and capital goods (human-made tools and equipment.)
    a. Product Pipeline   b. Long-run
    c. Hicks-neutral technical change   d. Factors of production

4. _____ is the term denoting either an entrance or changes which are inserted into a system and which activate/modify a process. It is an abstract concept, used in the modeling, system(s) design and system(s) exploitation. It is usually connected with other terms, e.g., _____ field, _____ variable, _____ parameter, _____ value, _____ signal, _____ device and _____ file.
    a. ACCRA Cost of Living Index   b. ACEA agreement
    c. AD-IA Model   d. Input

5.   Competitive market equilibrium is the traditional concept of economic equilibrium, appropriate for the analysis of commodity markets with flexible prices and many traders, and serving as the benchmark of efficiency in economic analysis. It relies crucially on the assumption of a competitive environment where each trader decides upon a quantity that is so small compared to the total quantity traded in the market that their individual transactions have no influence on the prices.Competitive markets are an ideal, a standard that other market structures are evaluated by.

A _____ consists of a vector of prices and an allocation such that given the prices, each trader by maximizing his objective function (profit, preferences) subject to his technological possibilities and resource constraints plans to trade into his part of the proposed allocation, and such that the prices make all net trades compatible with one another ('clear the market') by equating aggregate supply and demand for the commodities which are traded.

a. Partial equilibrium   b. Market system
c. Competitive equilibrium   d. Product-Market Growth Matrix

6.   In economics, the _____ or marginal physical product is the extra output produced by one more unit of an input (for instance, the difference in output when a firm's labour is increased from five to six units.) Assuming that no other inputs to production change, the _____ of a given input (X) can be expressed as:

_____ = $\Delta Y/\Delta X$ = (the change of Y)/(the change of X.)

-
   ○
      ▪ Pending approval by Thomas Sowell***

In neoclassical economics, this is the mathematical derivative of the production function.... Note that the 'product' (Y) is typically defined ignoring external costs and benefits.

a. Factor prices   b. Labor problem
c. Marginal product   d. Productive capacity

7.   In economics, the _____ also known as MPL or MPN is the change in output from hiring one additional unit of labor. It is the increase in output added by the last unit of labor. Assuming that no other inputs to production change, the marginal product of a given input (X) can be expressed as:

MP = $\Delta Y/\Delta X$ = (the change of Y)/(the change of X.)

a. Marginal product   b. Production function
c. Marginal product of labor   d. Product Pipeline

8.   In economics, _____ refers to how the marginal contribution of a factor of production usually decreases as more of the factor is used. According to this relationship, in a production system with fixed and variable inputs, beyond some point, each additional unit of the variable input yields smaller and smaller increases in output. Conversely, producing one more unit of output costs more and more in variable inputs.

a. Community property   b. Derivatives law
c. Patent troll   d. Diminishing returns

9. _____ is generally measured by standards such as real (i.e. inflation adjusted) income per person and poverty rate. Other measures such as access and quality of health care, income growth inequality and educational standards are also used. Examples are access to certain goods (such as number of refrigerators per 1000 people), or measures of health such as life expectancy.

a. 100-year flood   b. Remuneration
c. 130-30 fund   d. Standard of living

10. _____ in economics refers to metrics and measures of output from production processes, per unit of input. Labor _____, for example, is typically measured as a ratio of output per labor-hour, an input. _____ may be conceived of as a metrics of the technical or engineering efficiency of production.

a. Piece work   b. Fordism
c. Production-possibility frontier   d. Productivity

11. _____ is a term that is used to describe the overall process of invention, innovation and diffusion of technology or processes. The term is redundant with technological development, technological achievement, and technological progress. In essence _____ is the invention of a technology (or a process), the continuous process of improving a technology (in which it often becomes cheaper) and its diffusion throughout industry or society.

a. 130-30 fund   b. 1921 recession
c. 100-year flood   d. Technological change

12. In economics, an _____ is a contour line drawn through the set of points at which the same quantity of output is produced while changing the quantities of two or more inputs. While an indifference curve helps to answer the utility-maximizing problem of consumers, the _____ deals with the cost-minimization problem of producers. _____s are typically drawn on capital-labor graphs, showing the tradeoff between capital and labor in the production function, and the decreasing marginal returns of both inputs.

a. Economic production quantity   b. Underinvestment employment relationship
c. Economies of scale   d. Isoquant

13. In economics, the _____ or the Technical Rate of Substitution (TRS) is the amount by which the quantity of one input has to be reduced ($- \Delta x_2$) when one extra unit of another input is used ($\Delta x_1 = 1$), so that output remains constant ($y = \bar{y}$.)

$$MRTS(x_1, x_2) = \frac{\Delta x_2}{\Delta x_1} = -\frac{MP_1}{MP_2}$$

where MP_1 and MP_2 are the marginal products of input 1 and input 2, respectively.

Along an isoquant, the MRTS shows the rate at which one input (e.g. capital or labor) may be substituted for another, while maintaining the same level of output.

a. Producer surplus

b. Pork cycle

c. Household production function

d. Marginal rate of technical substitution

14.   In economics, a _____ is a function that specifies the output of a firm, an industry, or an entire economy for all combinations of inputs. A meta-_____ compares the practice of the existing entities converting inputs X into output y to determine the most efficient practice _____ of the existing entities, whether the most efficient feasible practice production or the most efficient actual practice production. In either case, the maximum output of a technologically-determined production process is a mathematical function of input factors of production.

a. Constant elasticity of substitution

b. Short-run

c. Post-Fordism

d. Production function

15.   In economics, _____ is the total demand for final goods and services in the economy (Y) at a given time and price level. It is the amount of goods and services in the economy that will be purchased at all possible price levels. This is the demand for the gross domestic product of a country when inventory levels are static.

a. Aggregate supply

b. Aggregation problem

c. Aggregate expenditure

d. Aggregate demand

16.   Economics:

- _____,the desire to own something and the ability to pay for it
- _____ curve,a graphic representation of a _____ schedule
- _____ deposit, the money in checking accounts
- _____ pull theory,the theory that inflation occurs when _____ for goods and services exceeds existing supplies
- _____ schedule,a table that lists the quantity of a good a person will buy it each different price
- _____ side economics,the school of economics at believes government spending and tax cuts open economy by raising _____

a. McKesson ' Robbins scandal

b. Demand

c. Production

d. Variability

17.   In production, returns to scale refers to changes in output subsequent to a proportional change in all inputs (where all inputs increase by a constant factor.) If output increases by that same proportional change then there are _____ If output increases by less than that proportional change, there are decreasing returns to scale (DRS.)

a. Consumer sovereignty

b. Lexicographic preferences

c. Constant returns to scale

d. Long term

18.   In calculus, a function f defined on a subset of the real numbers with real values is called _____, if for all x and y such that x >≤ y one has f(x) >≤ f(y), so f preserves the order. In layman's terms, the sign of the slope is always positive (the curve tending upwards) or zero (i.e., non-decreasing, or asymptotic, or depicted as a horizontal, flat line) Likewise, a function is called monotonically decreasing (non-increasing) if, whenever x >≤ y, then f(x) >≥ f(y), so it reverses the order.

a. 130-30 fund

b. 100-year flood

c. 1921 recession

d. Monotonic

19. In economics, _____ and economies of scale are related terms that describe what happens as the scale of production increases. They are different terms and should not be used interchangeably.

_____ refers to a technical property of production that examines changes in output subsequent to a proportional change in all inputs (where all inputs increase by a constant factor.)

a. Constant returns to scale

b. Customer equity

c. Necessity good

d. Returns to scale

1. In microeconomics, _____ is quite simply the conversion of inputs into outputs. It is an economic process that uses resources to create a good or service that is suitable for exchange. This can include manufacturing, storing, shipping, and packaging.

   a. Solved
   b. MET
   c. Production
   d. Red Guards

2. In economics, the concept of the _____ refers to the decision-making time frame of a firm in which at least one factor of production is fixed. Costs which are fixed in the _____ have no impact on a firms decisions. For example a firm can raise output by increasing the amount of labour through overtime.

   a. Product Pipeline
   b. Hicks-neutral technical change
   c. Productivity model
   d. Short-run

3. _____s is the social science that studies the production, distribution, and consumption of goods and services. The term _____s comes from the Ancient Greek oá¼°κονομῑα from oá¼¶κος (oikos, 'house') + νΊμος (nomos, 'custom' or 'law'), hence 'rules of the house(hold)'. Current _____ models developed out of the broader field of political economy in the late 19th century, owing to a desire to use an empirical approach more akin to the physical sciences.

   a. Opportunity cost
   b. Energy economics
   c. Inflation
   d. Economic

4. The _____ of a decision depends on both the cost of the alternative chosen and the benefit that the best alternative would have provided if chosen. _____ differs from accounting cost because it includes opportunity cost.

   a. Inventory analysis
   b. Epstein-Zin preferences
   c. Economic cost
   d. Isocost

5. _____ or economic opportunity loss is the value of the next best alternative foregone as the result of making a decision. _____ analysis is an important part of a company's decision-making processes but is not treated as an actual cost in any financial statement. The next best thing that a person can engage in is referred to as the _____ of doing the best thing and ignoring the next best thing to be done.

   a. Opportunity cost
   b. Industrial organization
   c. Economic
   d. Economic ideology

6. In economics, _____ are business expenses that are not dependent on the activities of the business They tend to be time-related, such as salaries or rents being paid per month. This is in contrast to variable costs, which are volume-related (and are paid per quantity.)

   In management accounting, _____ are defined as expenses that do not change in proportion to the activity of a business, within the relevant period or scale of production.

   a. Quality costs
   b. Cost of poor quality
   c. Cost-Volume-Profit Analysis
   d. Fixed costs

7. In economics, and cost accounting, _____ describes the total economic cost of production and is made up of variable costs, which vary according to the quantity of a good produced and include inputs such as labor and raw materials, plus fixed costs, which are independent of the quantity of a good produced and include inputs (capital) that cannot be varied in the short term, such as buildings and machinery. _____ in economics includes the total opportunity cost of each factor of production in addition to fixed and variable costs.

The rate at which _____ changes as the amount produced changes is called marginal cost.

a. 100-year flood   b. Total cost
c. 1921 recession   d. 130-30 fund

8.   _____s are expenses that change in proportion to the activity of a business. In other words, _____ is the sum of marginal costs. It can also be considered normal costs.

a. Cost allocation   b. Quality costs
c. Variable cost   d. Cost-Volume-Profit Analysis

9.   The _____ consists of a number of economic theories which describe the nature of the firm, company including its existence, its behaviour, and its relationship with the market.

In simplified terms, the _____ aims to answer these questions:

1.   Existence - why do firms emerge, why are not all transactions in the economy mediated over the market?
2.   Boundaries - why the boundary between firms and the market is located exactly there? Which transactions are performed internally and which are negotiated on the market?
3.   Organization - why are firms structured in such specific way? What is the interplay of formal and informal relationships?

Despite looking simple, these questions are not answered by the established economic theory, which usually views firms as given, and treats them as black boxes without any internal structure.

The First World War period saw a change of emphasis in economic theory away from industry-level analysis which mainly included analysing markets to analysis at the level of the firm, as it became increasingly clear that perfect competition was no longer an adequate model of how firms behaved. Economic theory till then had focussed on trying to understand markets alone and there had been little study on understanding why firms or organisations exist.

a. Technology gap   b. Policy Ineffectiveness Proposition
c. Khazzoom-Brookes postulate   d. Theory of the firm

10.   In economics and business decision-making, _____ are costs that cannot be recovered once they have been incurred. _____ are sometimes contrasted with variable costs, which are the costs that will change due to the proposed course of action, and prospective costs which are costs that will be incurred if an action is taken.

In traditional microeconomic theory, only variable costs are relevant to a decision.

a. Hyperbolic discounting   b. Halo effect
c. Post-purchase rationalization   d. Sunk costs

11.   In economics and finance, _____ is the change in total cost that arises when the quantity produced changes by one unit. It is the cost of producing one more unit of a good. Mathematically, the _____ function is expressed as the first derivative of the total cost (TC) function with respect to quantity (Q.)

a. Variable cost   b. Quality costs

c. Khozraschyot   d. Marginal cost

12.   _____ is an economics term used to describe the total fixed costs (TFC) divided by the quantity (Q) of units produced.

$$AFC = \frac{TFC}{Q}$$

_____ is a per-unit measure of fixed costs. As the total number of goods produced increases, the _____ decreases because the same amount of fixed costs are being spread over a larger number of units.

a. Inventory valuation   b. Average variable cost

c. Explicit cost   d. Average fixed cost

13.   _____ is an economics term to describe a firms variable costs (labor, electricity, etc.) divided by the quantity (Q) of total units of output.

$$AVC = \frac{TVC}{Q}$$

Where:

- TVC = Total Variable Cost
- _____ = Average variable cost
- Q = Quantity of Units Produced

_____ plus average fixed cost equals average total cost:

_____ + AFC = ATC.

a. Average variable cost   b. Average fixed cost

c. Inventory valuation   d. Explicit cost

14.   In algebra, a _____ is a function depending on n that associates a scalar, det(A), to an n×n square matrix A. The fundamental geometric meaning of a _____ is a scale factor for measure when A is regarded as a linear transformation. _____s are important both in calculus, where they enter the substitution rule for several variables, and in multilinear algebra.

For a fixed nonnegative integer n, there is a unique _____ function for the n×n matrices over any commutative ring R. In particular, this function exists when R is the field of real or complex numbers.

a. Determinant

b. 1921 recession

c. 130-30 fund

d. 100-year flood

15.   In economics, a _____ is a graph of the costs of production as a function of total quantity produced. In a free market economy, productively efficient firms use these curves to find the optimal point of production, where they make the most profits. There are a few different types of _____s, each relevant to a different area of economics.

a. Phillips curve

b. Cost curve

c. Demand curve

d. Kuznets curve

16.   In economics, _____ refers to how the marginal contribution of a factor of production usually decreases as more of the factor is used. According to this relationship, in a production system with fixed and variable inputs, beyond some point, each additional unit of the variable input yields smaller and smaller increases in output. Conversely, producing one more unit of output costs more and more in variable inputs.

a. Community property

b. Patent troll

c. Derivatives law

d. Diminishing returns

17.   In economic models, the _____ time frame assumes no fixed factors of production. Firms can enter or leave the marketplace, and the cost (and availability) of land, labor, raw materials, and capital goods can be assumed to vary. In contrast, in the short-run time frame, certain factors are assumed to be fixed, because there is not sufficient time for them to change.

a. Diseconomies of scale

b. Price/performance ratio

c. Long-run

d. Productivity world

18.   The _____ is an expected return that the provider of capital plans to earn on their investment.

Capital (money) used for funding a business should earn returns for the capital providers who risk their capital. For an investment to be worthwhile, the expected return on capital must be greater than the _____.

a. Capital expenditure

b. Capital intensive

c. Modigliani-Miller theorem

d. Cost of Capital

19.   _____ is the term denoting either an entrance or changes which are inserted into a system and which activate/modify a process. It is an abstract concept, used in the modeling, system(s) design and system(s) exploitation. It is usually connected with other terms, e.g., _____ field, _____ variable, _____ parameter, _____ value, _____ signal, _____ device and _____ file.

a. ACCRA Cost of Living Index

b. Input

c. AD-IA Model

d. ACEA agreement

20.   _____ in economics and business is the result of an exchange and from that trade we assign a numerical monetary value to a good, service or asset. If Alice trades Bob 4 apples for an orange, the _____ of an orange is 4 apples. Inversely, the _____ of an apple is 1/4 oranges.

a. Premium pricing

b. Price war

c. Price book

d. Price

21. In economics an _____ line represents a combination of inputs which all cost the same amount. Although similar to the budget constraint in consumer theory, the use of the _____ pertains to cost-minimization in production, as opposed to utility-maximization. The typical _____ line represents the ratio of costs of labour and capital, so the formula is often written as:

$$rK + wL = C$$

Where w represents the wage of labour, and r represents the rental rate of capital.

a. Incentive

c. Inventory analysis

b. Epstein-Zin preferences

d. Isocost

22. _____ is a practice of protecting the environment, on individual, organisational or governmental level, for the benefit of the natural environment and (or) humans.

Due to the pressures of population and technology the biophysical environment is being degraded, sometimes permanently. This has been recognised and governments began placing restraints on activities that caused environmental degradation.

a. Environmental Protection

c. AD-IA Model

b. ACCRA Cost of Living Index

d. ACEA agreement

23. Under the system of feudalism, a _____, fief, feud, feoff often consisted of inheritable lands or revenue-producing property granted by a liege lord, generally to a vassal, in return for a form of allegiance, originally to give him the means to fulfill his military duties when called upon. However anything of value could be held in fief, such as an office, a right of exploitation (e.g., hunting, fishing) or any other type of revenue, rather than the land it comes from.

Originally, the feudal institution of vassalage did not imply the giving or receiving of landholdings (which were granted only as a reward for loyalty), but by the eighth century the giving of a landholding was becoming standard.

a. 1921 recession

c. 100-year flood

b. Fiefdom

d. 130-30 fund

24. In economics, _____ is equal to total cost divided by the number of goods produced (the output quantity, Q.) It is also equal to the sum of average variable costs (total variable costs divided by Q) plus average fixed costs (total fixed costs divided by Q.) _____s may be dependent on the time period considered (increasing production may be expensive or impossible in the short term, for example.)

a. Average cost

c. Explicit cost

b. Average fixed cost

d. Average variable cost

25. In production, returns to scale refers to changes in output subsequent to a proportional change in all inputs (where all inputs increase by a constant factor.) If output increases by that same proportional change then there are _____ If output increases by less than that proportional change, there are decreasing returns to scale (DRS.)

a. Constant returns to scale
c. Long term

b. Lexicographic preferences
d. Consumer sovereignty

26. _____ are the forces that cause larger firms to produce goods and services at increased per-unit costs. They are less well known than what economists have long understood as 'economies of scale', the forces which enable larger firms to produce goods and services at reduced per-unit costs.

Some of the forces which cause a diseconomy of scale are listed below:

Ideally, all employees of a firm would have one-on-one communication with each other so they know exactly what the other workers are doing.

a. Marginal physical product
c. Diseconomies of scale

b. Factors of production
d. Productive capacity

27. _____, in microeconomics, are the cost advantages that a business obtains due to expansion. They are factors that cause a producere;s average cost per unit to fall as scale is increased. _____ is a long run concept and refers to reductions in unit cost as the size of a facility, or scale, increases.

a. Isoquant
c. Economic production quantity

b. Underinvestment employment relationship
d. Economies of scale

28. In economics, _____ and economies of scale are related terms that describe what happens as the scale of production increases. They are different terms and should not be used interchangeably.

_____ refers to a technical property of production that examines changes in output subsequent to a proportional change in all inputs (where all inputs increase by a constant factor.)

a. Returns to scale
c. Customer equity

b. Necessity good
d. Constant returns to scale

29. In calculus, a function f defined on a subset of the real numbers with real values is called _____, if for all x and y such that x >≤ y one has f(x) >≤ f(y), so f preserves the order. In layman's terms, the sign of the slope is always positive (the curve tending upwards) or zero (i.e., non-decreasing, or asymptotic, or depicted as a horizontal, flat line) Likewise, a function is called monotonically decreasing (non-increasing) if, whenever x >≤ y, then f(x) >≥ f(y), so it reverses the order.

a. 130-30 fund
c. Monotonic

b. 1921 recession
d. 100-year flood

30. _____ are conceptually similar to economies of scale. Whereas economies of scale primarily refer to efficiencies associated with supply-side changes, such as increasing or decreasing the scale of production, of a single product type, _____ refer to efficiencies primarily associated with demand-side changes, such as increasing or decreasing the scope of marketing and distribution, of different types of products. _____ are one of the main reasons for such marketing strategies as product bundling, product lining, and family branding.

a. Economies of scale
c. Isoquant

b. Economies of scope
d. Economic production quantity

31. In economics, the _____ functional form of production functions is widely used to represent the relationship of an output to inputs. It was proposed by Knut Wicksell (1851-1926), and tested against statistical evidence by Charles Cobb and Paul Douglas in 1900-1928.

For production, the function is

$$Y = AL^{\alpha}K^{\beta},$$

where:

- Y = total production (the monetary value of all goods produced in a year)
- L = labor input
- K = capital input
- A = total factor productivity
- α and β are the output elasticities of labor and capital, respectively. These values are constants determined by available technology.

Output elasticity measures the responsiveness of output to a change in levels of either labor or capital used in production, ceteris paribus. For example if α = 0.15, a 1% increase in labor would lead to approximately a 0.15% increase in output.

a. Growth accounting

b. Demand-pull theory

c. Social savings

d. Cobb-Douglas

32. Network externalities resemble economies of scale, but they are not considered such because they are a function of the number of users of a good or service in an industry, not of the production efficiency within a business. _____ are only considered examples of network externalities if they are driven by demand side economies.

Formally, a production function $F(K, L)$ is defined to have:

- constant returns to scale if (for any constant a greater than or equal to 0) $F(aK, aL) = aF(K, L)$
- increasing returns to scale if (for any constant a greater than 1) $F(aK, aL) > aF(K, L),$
- decreasing returns to scale if (for any constant a greater than 1) $F(aK, aL) < aF(K, L)$

where K and L are factors of production, capital and labour, respectively.

As an example, the Cobb-Douglas functional form has constant returns to scale when the sum of the exponents adds up to one.

a. Economies of scale external to the firm

b. ACCRA Cost of Living Index

c. AD-IA Model

d. ACEA agreement

33. A _____ association is a financial institution that specializes in accepting savings deposits and making mortgage and other loans. The S'L or thrift term is mainly used in the United States; similar institutions in the United Kingdom, Ireland and some Commonwealth countries include building societies and trustee savings banks.

They are often mutually held, meaning that the depositors and borrowers are members with voting rights, and have the ability to direct the financial and managerial goals of the organization, similar to the policyholders of a mutual insurance company.

a. Fonds commun de placement

b. Collective investment scheme

c. Participating policy

d. Savings and loan

34. A _____ is one scenario provided for evaluation by respondents in a Choice Experiment. Responses are collected and used to create a Choice Model. Respondents are usually provided with a series of differing _____s for evaluation.

a. 1921 recession

b. Choice Set

c. 130-30 fund

d. 100-year flood

35. In economics, an _____ is a contour line drawn through the set of points at which the same quantity of output is produced while changing the quantities of two or more inputs. While an indifference curve helps to answer the utility-maximizing problem of consumers, the _____ deals with the cost-minimization problem of producers. _____s are typically drawn on capital-labor graphs, showing the tradeoff between capital and labor in the production function, and the decreasing marginal returns of both inputs.

a. Economic production quantity

b. Underinvestment employment relationship

c. Isoquant

d. Economies of scale

36. In economics, the _____ or the Technical Rate of Substitution (TRS) is the amount by which the quantity of one input has to be reduced ($-\Delta x_2$) when one extra unit of another input is used ($\Delta x_1 = 1$), so that output remains constant ($y = \bar{y}_)$

$$MRTS(x_1, x_2) = \frac{\Delta x_2}{\Delta x_1} = -\frac{MP_1}{MP_2}$$

where MP_1 and MP_2 are the marginal products of input 1 and input 2, respectively.

Along an isoquant, the MRTS shows the rate at which one input (e.g. capital or labor) may be substituted for another, while maintaining the same level of output.

a. Pork cycle

b. Household production function

c. Marginal rate of technical substitution

d. Producer surplus

37. In economics, _____ is a measure of the relative satisfaction from consumption of various goods and services. Given this measure, one may speak meaningfully of increasing or decreasing _____, and thereby explain economic behavior in terms of attempts to increase one's _____. For illustrative purposes, changes in _____ are sometimes expressed in units called utils.

a. Utility function
c. Ordinal utility

b. Expected utility hypothesis
d. Utility

38.   While preferences are the conventional foundation of microeconomics, it is often convenient to represent preferences with a _____ and reason indirectly about preferences with _____s. Let X be the consumption set, the set of all mutually-exclusive packages the consumer could conceivably consume (such as an indifference curve map without the indifference curves.) The consumer's _____ $u : X \rightarrow \mathbf{R}$ ranks each package in the consumption set.

a. Expected utility hypothesis
c. Utility

b. Ordinal utility
d. Utility function

1. _____ is a term used by economists to describe a condition in which firms can freely enter the market for an economic good by establishing production and beginning to sell the product.

_____ is implied by the perfect competition condition that there is an unlimited number of buyers and sellers in a market. In comparison to perfect competition, however, _____ is a condition often more applicable to real world conditions.

a. 100-year flood   b. Free entry
c. 1921 recession   d. 130-30 fund

2. _____ is an economic concept with commonplace familiarity. It is the price that a good or service is offered at, or will fetch, in the marketplace. It is of interest mainly in the study of microeconomics.

a. Market price   b. Noisy market hypothesis
c. Paper trading   d. Market anomaly

3. _____ in economics and business is the result of an exchange and from that trade we assign a numerical monetary value to a good, service or asset. If Alice trades Bob 4 apples for an orange, the _____ of an orange is 4 apples. Inversely, the _____ of an apple is 1/4 oranges.

a. Price book   b. Premium pricing
c. Price war   d. Price

4. In economics, _____ is the process by which a firm determines the price and output level that returns the greatest profit. There are several approaches to this problem. The total revenue--total cost method relies on the fact that profit equals revenue minus cost, and the marginal revenue--marginal cost method is based on the fact that total profit in a perfectly competitive market reaches its maximum point where marginal revenue equals marginal cost.

a. Profit margin   b. Normal profit
c. 100-year flood   d. Profit maximization

5. In economics and finance, _____ is the change in total cost that arises when the quantity produced changes by one unit. It is the cost of producing one more unit of a good. Mathematically, the _____ function is expressed as the first derivative of the total cost (TC) function with respect to quantity (Q.)

a. Variable cost   b. Quality costs
c. Khozraschyot   d. Marginal cost

6. In microeconomics, _____ is the extra revenue that an additional unit of product will bring. It is the additional income from selling one more unit of a good; sometimes equal to price. It can also be described as the change in total revenue/change in number of units sold.

a. Marginal revenue   b. Long term
c. Reservation price   d. Market demand schedule

7. _____s is the social science that studies the production, distribution, and consumption of goods and services. The term _____s comes from the Ancient Greek oἰκονομῑ α from oἰκος (oikos, 'house') + vῐΈμος (nomos, 'custom' or 'law'), hence 'rules of the house(hold)'. Current _____ models developed out of the broader field of political economy in the late 19th century, owing to a desire to use an empirical approach more akin to the physical sciences.

a. Inflation   b. Economic
c. Opportunity cost   d. Energy economics

8.   Economics:

- _____,the desire to own something and the ability to pay for it
- _____ curve,a graphic representation of a _____ schedule
- _____ deposit, the money in checking accounts
- _____ pull theory,the theory that inflation occurs when _____ for goods and services exceeds existing supplies
- _____ schedule,a table that lists the quantity of a good a person will buy it each different price
- _____ side economics,the school of economics at believes government spending and tax cuts open economy by raising _____

a. Demand

c. Variability

b. McKesson ' Robbins scandal

d. Production

9.   In economics, the _____ can be defined as the graph depicting the relationship between the price of a certain commodity, and the amount of it that consumers are willing and able to purchase at that given price. It is a graphic representation of a demand schedule. The _____ for all consumers together follows from the _____ of every individual consumer: the individual demands at each price are added together.

a. Wage curve

c. Cost curve

b. Demand curve

d. Kuznets curve

10.   In economics, the concept of the _____ refers to the decision-making time frame of a firm in which at least one factor of production is fixed. Costs which are fixed in the _____ have no impact on a firms decisions. For example a firm can raise output by increasing the amount of labour through overtime.

a. Short-run

c. Hicks-neutral technical change

b. Product Pipeline

d. Productivity model

11. A _____ is:

- Rewrite _____, in generative grammar and computer science
- Standardization, a formal and widely-accepted statement, fact, definition, or qualification
- Operation, a determinate _____ for performing a mathematical operation and obtaining a certain result (Mathematics, Logic)
    - Unary operation
    - Binary operation
- _____ of inference, a function from sets of formulae to formulae (Mathematics, Logic)
- _____ of thumb, principle with broad application that is not intended to be strictly accurate or reliable for every situation. Also often simply referred to as a _____
- Moral, an atomic element of a moral code for guiding choices in human behavior
- Heuristic, a quantized '_____' which shows a tendency or probability for successful function
- A regulation, as in sports
- A Production _____, as in computer science
- Procedural law, a _____ set governing the application of laws to cases
    - A law, which may informally be called a '_____'
    - A court ruling, a decision by a court
- In the U.S. Government, a regulation mandated by Congress, but written or expanded upon by the Executive Branch.
- Norm (sociology), an informal but widely accepted _____, concept, truth, definition, or qualification (social norms, legal norms, coding norms)
- Norm (philosophy), a kind of sentence or a reason to act, feel or believe
- 'Rulership' is the concept of governance by a government:
    - Military _____, governance by a military body
    - Monastic _____, a collection of precepts that guides the life of monks or nuns in a religious order where the superior holds the place of Christ
- Slide _____

- '_____,' a song by Ayumi Hamasaki
- '_____,' a song by rapper Nas
- '_____s,' an album by the band The Whitest Boy Alive
- _____s: Pyaar Ka Superhit Formula, a 2003 Bollywood film
- ruler, an instrument for measuring lengths
- _____, a component of an astrolabe, circumferator or similar instrument
- The _____s, a bestselling self-help book
- _____ Project (Run Up-to-date Linux Everywhere), a project that aims to use up-to-date Linux software on old PCs
- _____ engine, a software system that helps managing business _____s
- Ja _____, a hip hop artist
    - R.U.L.E., a 2005 greatest hits album by rapper Ja _____
- '_____s,' a KMFDM song

a. Technocracy   b. Procter ' Gamble
c. Demand   d. Rule

12.   The _____ of a decision depends on both the cost of the alternative chosen and the benefit that the best alternative would have provided if chosen. _____ differs from accounting cost because it includes opportunity cost.
   a. Economic cost
   c. Inventory analysis
   b. Isocost
   d. Epstein-Zin preferences

13.   In economics, _____ refers to how the marginal contribution of a factor of production usually decreases as more of the factor is used. According to this relationship, in a production system with fixed and variable inputs, beyond some point, each additional unit of the variable input yields smaller and smaller increases in output. Conversely, producing one more unit of output costs more and more in variable inputs.
   a. Patent troll
   c. Derivatives law
   b. Community property
   d. Diminishing returns

14.   _____ is the term denoting either an entrance or changes which are inserted into a system and which activate/modify a process. It is an abstract concept, used in the modeling, system(s) design and system(s) exploitation. It is usually connected with other terms, e.g., _____ field, _____ variable, _____ parameter, _____ value, _____ signal, _____ device and _____ file.
   a. ACCRA Cost of Living Index
   c. AD-IA Model
   b. ACEA agreement
   d. Input

15.   _____ describes a deliberate attempt to interfere with the free and fair operation of the market and create artificial, false or misleading appearances with respect to the price of a security, commodity or currency. _____ is prohibited under Section 9(a)(2) of the Securities Exchange Act of 1934, and in Australia under Section s 1041A of the Corporations Act 2001. The Act defines _____ as transactions which create an artificial price or maintain an artificial price for a tradable security.
   a. Net domestic product
   c. Market manipulation
   b. Legal monopoly
   d. Managerial economics

16.   In microeconomics, _____ is quite simply the conversion of inputs into outputs. It is an economic process that uses resources to create a good or service that is suitable for exchange. This can include manufacturing, storing, shipping, and packaging.
   a. Solved
   c. MET
   b. Red Guards
   d. Production

17.   In economics, _____ is the ratio of the percent change in one variable to the percent change in another variable. It is a tool for measuring the responsiveness of a function to changes in parameters in a relative way. Commonly analyzed are _____ of substitution, price and wealth.
   a. Elasticity of demand
   c. ACEA agreement
   b. ACCRA Cost of Living Index
   d. Elasticity

18.   In economics, _____ describes demand that is not very sensitive to a change in price.
   a. Effective unemployment rate
   c. Export-led growth
   b. Inflation hedge
   d. Inelastic

19.   The _____ consists of a number of economic theories which describe the nature of the firm, company including its existence, its behaviour, and its relationship with the market.

In simplified terms, the _____ aims to answer these questions:

1. Existence - why do firms emerge, why are not all transactions in the economy mediated over the market?
2. Boundaries - why the boundary between firms and the market is located exactly there? Which transactions are performed internally and which are negotiated on the market?
3. Organization - why are firms structured in such specific way? What is the interplay of formal and informal relationships?

Despite looking simple, these questions are not answered by the established economic theory, which usually views firms as given, and treats them as black boxes without any internal structure.

The First World War period saw a change of emphasis in economic theory away from industry-level analysis which mainly included analysing markets to analysis at the level of the firm, as it became increasingly clear that perfect competition was no longer an adequate model of how firms behaved. Economic theory till then had focussed on trying to understand markets alone and there had been little study on understanding why firms or organisations exist.

a. Policy Ineffectiveness Proposition   b. Khazzoom-Brookes postulate
c. Technology gap   d. Theory of the firm

20. _____ is a common concept in economics, and gives rise to derived concepts such as consumer debt. Generally _____ is defined by opposition to production. But the precise definition can vary because different schools of economists define production quite differently.
a. Consumption   b. Foreclosure data providers
c. Federal Reserve Bank Notes   d. Cash or share options

21. _____ is a broad label that refers to any individuals or households that use goods and services generated within the economy. The concept of a _____ is used in different contexts, so that the usage and significance of the term may vary.

Typically when business people and economists talk of _____s they are talking about person as _____, an aggregated commodity item with little individuality other than that expressed in the buy/not-buy decision.

a. Consumer   b. 130-30 fund
c. 100-year flood   d. 1921 recession

22. The term surplus is used in economics for several related quantities. The _____ is the amount that consumers benefit by being able to purchase a product for a price that is less than they would be willing to pay. The producer surplus is the amount that producers benefit by selling at a market price mechanism that is higher than they would be willing to sell for.
a. Necessity good   b. Marginal rate of technical substitution
c. Microeconomic reform   d. Consumer surplus

23.   The term surplus is used in economics for several related quantities. The consumer surplus is the amount that consumers benefit by being able to purchase a product for a price that is less than they would be willing to pay. The _____ is the amount that producers benefit by selling at a market price mechanism that is higher than they would be willing to sell for.

a. Producer surplus

b. Long term

c. Schedule delay

d. Returns to scale

24.   In economics, _____ is the difference between a company's total revenue and its opportunity costs. It is the increase in wealth that an investor has from making an investment, taking into consideration all costs associated with that investment including the opportunity cost of capital.

Profit is the factor income of the entrepreneur.

a. ACCRA Cost of Living Index

b. Accounting profit

c. Operating profit

d. Economic Profit

25.   Competitive market equilibrium is the traditional concept of economic equilibrium, appropriate for the analysis of commodity markets with flexible prices and many traders, and serving as the benchmark of efficiency in economic analysis. It relies crucially on the assumption of a competitive environment where each trader decides upon a quantity that is so small compared to the total quantity traded in the market that their individual transactions have no influence on the prices.Competitive markets are an ideal, a standard that other market structures are evaluated by.

A _____ consists of a vector of prices and an allocation such that given the prices, each trader by maximizing his objective function (profit, preferences) subject to his technological possibilities and resource constraints plans to trade into his part of the proposed allocation, and such that the prices make all net trades compatible with one another ('clear the market') by equating aggregate supply and demand for the commodities which are traded.

a. Market system

b. Partial equilibrium

c. Product-Market Growth Matrix

d. Competitive equilibrium

26.   _____, in microeconomics, are the cost advantages that a business obtains due to expansion. They are factors that cause a producere;s average cost per unit to fall as scale is increased. _____ is a long run concept and refers to reductions in unit cost as the size of a facility, or scale, increases.

a. Isoquant

b. Underinvestment employment relationship

c. Economic production quantity

d. Economies of scale

27.   _____ is the difference between price and the costs of bringing to market whatever it is that is accounted as an enterprise (whether by harvest, extraction, manufacture, or purchase) in terms of the component costs of delivered goods and/or services and any operating or other expenses.

A key difficulty in measuring profit is in defining costs. Pure economic monetary profits can be zero or negative even in competitive equilibrium when accounted monetized costs exceed monetized price.

a. Operating profit

b. Accounting profit

c. Economic profit

d. ACCRA Cost of Living Index

28. In economic models, the _____ time frame assumes no fixed factors of production. Firms can enter or leave the marketplace, and the cost (and availability) of land, labor, raw materials, and capital goods can be assumed to vary. In contrast, in the short-run time frame, certain factors are assumed to be fixed, because there is not sufficient time for them to change.

a. Price/performance ratio

b. Productivity world

c. Diseconomies of scale

d. Long-run

29. _____ or economic opportunity loss is the value of the next best alternative foregone as the result of making a decision. _____ analysis is an important part of a company's decision-making processes but is not treated as an actual cost in any financial statement. The next best thing that a person can engage in is referred to as the _____ of doing the best thing and ignoring the next best thing to be done.

a. Economic

b. Industrial organization

c. Economic ideology

d. Opportunity cost

30. In economics supernormal profit _____ or pure profit or excess profits, is a profit exceeding the normal profit. Normal profit equals the opportunity cost of labour and capital, while supernormal profit is the amount exceeds the normal return from these input factors in production.

_____ is usually generated by an oligopoly or a monopoly; however, these firms often try to hide this from the market to reduce risk of competition or antitrust investigation.

a. Abnormal profit

b. Accounting profit

c. Economic profit

d. ACCRA Cost of Living Index

31. Economic _____ is defined as an excess distribution to any factor in a production process above that which is required to induce the factor into the process or any excess above that which is necessary to keep the factor in its current use..

Classical Factor _____ is primarily concerned with the fee paid for the use of fixed (e.g. natural) resources. The classical definition is expressed as any excess payment above that required to induce or provide for production.

a. 1921 recession

b. 130-30 fund

c. 100-year flood

d. Rent

32. In calculus, a function f defined on a subset of the real numbers with real values is called _____, if for all x and y such that $x \geq y$ one has $f(x) \geq f(y)$, so f preserves the order. In layman's terms, the sign of the slope is always positive (the curve tending upwards) or zero (i.e., non-decreasing, or asymptotic, or depicted as a horizontal, flat line) Likewise, a function is called monotonically decreasing (non-increasing) if, whenever $x \geq y$, then $f(x) \geq f(y)$, so it reverses the order.

a. 1921 recession

b. 130-30 fund

c. 100-year flood

d. Monotonic

33. To _____ is to impose a financial charge or other levy upon a taxpayer by a state or the functional equivalent of a state.

_____es are also imposed by many subnational entities. _____es consist of direct _____ or indirect _____, and may be paid in money or as its labour equivalent (often but not always unpaid.)

a. 130-30 fund   b. Tax
c. 1921 recession   d. 100-year flood

34. A _____ is a price discrimination technique in which the price of a product or service is composed of two parts - a lump-sum fee as well as a per-unit charge. In general, price discrimination techniques only occur in partially or fully monopolistic markets. It is designed to enable the firm to capture more consumer surplus than it otherwise would in a non-discriminating pricing environment.

a. Price floor   b. Big ticket item
c. Two-part tariff   d. Penetration pricing

35. A _____ is a duty imposed on goods when they are moved across a political boundary. They are usually associated with protectionism, the economic policy of restraining trade between nations. For political reasons, _____s are usually imposed on imported goods, although they may also be imposed on exported goods.

a. 100-year flood   b. 130-30 fund
c. 1921 recession   d. Tariff

36. In economics, the _____ is defined as a numerical measure of the responsiveness of the quantity supplied of product (A) to a change in price of product (A) alone. It is the measure of the way quantity supplied reacts to a change in price.

For example, if, in response to a 10% rise in the price of a good, the quantity supplied increases by 20%, the _____ would be 20%/10% = 2.

a. Passive income   b. Hedonimetry
c. Demand shaping   d. Price elasticity of supply

1. _____ in economics and business is the result of an exchange and from that trade we assign a numerical monetary value to a good, service or asset. If Alice trades Bob 4 apples for an orange, the _____ of an orange is 4 apples. Inversely, the _____ of an apple is 1/4 oranges.

   a. Price war
   c. Premium pricing

   b. Price book
   d. Price

2. _____ is a broad label that refers to any individuals or households that use goods and services generated within the economy. The concept of a _____ is used in different contexts, so that the usage and significance of the term may vary.

   Typically when business people and economists talk of _____s they are talking about person as _____, an aggregated commodity item with little individuality other than that expressed in the buy/not-buy decision.

   a. 130-30 fund
   c. Consumer

   b. 100-year flood
   d. 1921 recession

3. The term surplus is used in economics for several related quantities. The _____ is the amount that consumers benefit by being able to purchase a product for a price that is less than they would be willing to pay. The producer surplus is the amount that producers benefit by selling at a market price mechanism that is higher than they would be willing to sell for.

   a. Necessity good
   c. Consumer surplus

   b. Marginal rate of technical substitution
   d. Microeconomic reform

4. The term surplus is used in economics for several related quantities. The consumer surplus is the amount that consumers benefit by being able to purchase a product for a price that is less than they would be willing to pay. The _____ is the amount that producers benefit by selling at a market price mechanism that is higher than they would be willing to sell for.

   a. Returns to scale
   c. Schedule delay

   b. Long term
   d. Producer surplus

5. In economics, a _____ is a loss of economic efficiency that can occur when equilibrium for a good or service is not Pareto optimal. In other words, either people who would have more marginal benefit than marginal cost are not buying the good or service, or people who would have more marginal cost than marginal benefit are buying the product.

   Causes of _____ can include monopoly pricing, externalities, taxes or subsidies, and binding price ceilings or floors.

   a. Contract curve
   c. Deadweight loss

   b. Distributive efficiency
   d. Leapfrogging

6. _____s is the social science that studies the production, distribution, and consumption of goods and services. The term _____s comes from the Ancient Greek οá¼°κονομῖα from οá¼¶κος (oikos, 'house') + νῖŒμος (nomos, 'custom' or 'law'), hence 'rules of the house(hold)'. Current _____ models developed out of the broader field of political economy in the late 19th century, owing to a desire to use an empirical approach more akin to the physical sciences.

   a. Energy economics
   c. Inflation

   b. Opportunity cost
   d. Economic

7. _____ is used to refer to a number of related concepts. It is the using resources in such a way as to maximize the production of goods and services. A system can be called economically efficient if:

- No one can be made better off without making someone else worse off.
- More output cannot be obtained without increasing the amount of inputs.
- Production proceeds at the lowest possible per-unit cost.

These definitions of efficiency are not equivalent, but they are all encompassed by the idea that nothing more can be achieved given the resources available.

An economic system is more efficient if it can provide more goods and services for society without using more resources.

a. Efficient contract theory
c. ACEA agreement

b. ACCRA Cost of Living Index
d. Economic efficiency

8. In economics, an _____ or spillover of an economic transaction is an impact on a party that is not directly involved in the transaction. In such a case, prices do not reflect the full costs or benefits in production or consumption of a product or service. A positive impact is called an external benefit, while a negative impact is called an external cost.

a. Environmental tariff
c. Environmental impact assessment

b. Externality
d. Existence value

9. In economics, a _____ exists when the production or use of goods and services by the market is not efficient. That is, there exists another outcome where all involved can be made better off. _____s can be viewed as scenarios where individuals' pursuit of pure self-interest leads to results that are not efficient - that can be improved upon from the societal point-of-view.

a. Financial economics
c. Fixed exchange rate

b. General equilibrium
d. Market failure

10. A _____ is a government imposed limit on how high a price can be charged on a product. For a _____ to be effective, it must differ from the free market price. In the graph at right, the supply and demand curves intersect to determine the free-market quantity and price.

a. Price ceiling
c. Fire sale

b. Product sabotage
d. Pricing

11. In economics, and cost accounting, _____ describes the total economic cost of production and is made up of variable costs, which vary according to the quantity of a good produced and include inputs such as labor and raw materials, plus fixed costs, which are independent of the quantity of a good produced and include inputs (capital) that cannot be varied in the short term, such as buildings and machinery. _____ in economics includes the total opportunity cost of each factor of production in addition to fixed and variable costs.

The rate at which _____ changes as the amount produced changes is called marginal cost.

a. 100-year flood
c. 1921 recession

b. 130-30 fund
d. Total cost

12.   A _____ is the lowest hourly, daily or monthly wage that employers may legally pay to employees or workers. Equivalently, it is the lowest wage at which workers may sell their labor. Although _____ laws are in effect in a great many jurisdictions, there are differences of opinion about the benefits and drawbacks of a _____.
   a. Marginal propensity to consume
   b. Permanent war economy
   c. Microfoundations
   d. Minimum wage

13.   In 1940, President Franklin Roosevelt split the authority into two agencies, the Civil Aeronautics Administration (CAA) and the _____ The CAA was responsible for air traffic control, safety programs, and airway development. The _____ was entrusted with safety rulemaking, accident investigation, and economic regulation of the airlines.
   a. 100-year flood
   b. 130-30 fund
   c. Civil Aeronautics Board
   d. 1921 recession

14.   In economics, a _____ may be either a subsidy or a price control, both with the intended effect of keeping the market price of a good higher than the competitive equilibrium level.

In the case of a price control, a _____ is the minimum legal price a seller may charge, typically placed above equilibrium. It is the support of certain price levels at or above market values by the government.

   a. Labor intensity
   b. Marginal profit
   c. Payment schedule
   d. Price support

15.   _____ is the study of when, why, how, where and what people do or do not buy products. It blends elements from psychology, sociology,social psychology, anthropology and economics. It attempts to understand the buyer decision making process, both individually and in groups.
   a. Shopping Neutral
   b. Consumer behavior
   c. Situational theory of publics
   d. Consumption smoothing

16.   In microeconomics, _____ is quite simply the conversion of inputs into outputs. It is an economic process that uses resources to create a good or service that is suitable for exchange. This can include manufacturing, storing, shipping, and packaging.
   a. Red Guards
   b. Solved
   c. Production
   d. MET

17.   In economics, an _____ is any good (e.g. a commodity) or service brought into one country from another country in a legitimate fashion, typically for use in trade.It is a good that is brought in from another country for sale. _____ goods or services are provided to domestic consumers by foreign producers. An _____ in the receiving country is an export to the sending country.
   a. Import
   b. Economic integration
   c. Incoterms
   d. Import quota

18.   In economics and sociology, an _____ is any factor (financial or non-financial) that enables or motivates a particular course of action, or counts as a reason for preferring one choice to the alternatives. It is an expectation that encourages people to behave in a certain way. Since human beings are purposeful creatures, the study of _____ structures is central to the study of all economic activity (both in terms of individual decision-making and in terms of co-operation and competition within a larger institutional structure.)

a. Economic reform
c. Isocost

b. Epstein-Zin preferences
d. Incentive

19. In economics, _____ is the total demand for final goods and services in the economy (Y) at a given time and price level. It is the amount of goods and services in the economy that will be purchased at all possible price levels. This is the demand for the gross domestic product of a country when inventory levels are static.

a. Aggregate demand
c. Aggregate expenditure

b. Aggregate supply
d. Aggregation problem

20. Economics:

- _____,the desire to own something and the ability to pay for it
- _____ curve,a graphic representation of a _____ schedule
- _____ deposit, the money in checking accounts
- _____ pull theory,the theory that inflation occurs when _____ for goods and services exceeds existing supplies
- _____ schedule,a table that lists the quantity of a good a person will buy it each different price
- _____ side economics,the school of economics at believes government spending and tax cuts open economy by raising _____

a. Production
c. McKesson ' Robbins scandal

b. Demand
d. Variability

21. _____ describes a deliberate attempt to interfere with the free and fair operation of the market and create artificial, false or misleading appearances with respect to the price of a security, commodity or currency. _____ is prohibited under Section 9(a)(2) of the Securities Exchange Act of 1934, and in Australia under Section s 1041A of the Corporations Act 2001. The Act defines _____ as transactions which create an artificial price or maintain an artificial price for a tradable security.

a. Net domestic product
c. Legal monopoly

b. Managerial economics
d. Market manipulation

22. An _____ is a type of protectionist trade restriction that sets a physical limit on the quantity of a good that can be imported into a country in a given period of time. Quotas, like other trade restrictions, are used to benefit the producers of a good in a domestic economy at the expense of all consumers of the good in that economy.

Critics say quotas often lead to corruption (bribes to get a quota allocation), smuggling (circumventing a quota), and higher prices for consumers.

a. Import quota
c. Agreement on Agriculture

b. Economic integration
d. International Monetary Systems

23. A _____ is a duty imposed on goods when they are moved across a political boundary. They are usually associated with protectionism, the economic policy of restraining trade between nations. For political reasons, _____s are usually imposed on imported goods, although they may also be imposed on exported goods.

a. Tariff   b. 100-year flood

c. 1921 recession   d. 130-30 fund

24.   To _____ is to impose a financial charge or other levy upon a taxpayer by a state or the functional equivalent of a state.

_____es are also imposed by many subnational entities. _____es consist of direct _____ or indirect _____, and may be paid in money or as its labour equivalent (often but not always unpaid.)

a. 100-year flood   b. 1921 recession

c. Tax   d. 130-30 fund

25.   A _____ is a price discrimination technique in which the price of a product or service is composed of two parts - a lump-sum fee as well as a per-unit charge. In general, price discrimination techniques only occur in partially or fully monopolistic markets. It is designed to enable the firm to capture more consumer surplus than it otherwise would in a non-discriminating pricing environment.

a. Big ticket item   b. Penetration pricing

c. Price floor   d. Two-part tariff

26.   A consumer price index (_____) is a measure of the average price of consumer goods and services purchased by households. A consumer price index measures a price change for a constant market basket of goods and services from one period to the next within the same area (city, region, or nation.) It is a price index determined by measuring the price of a standard group of goods meant to represent the typical market basket of a typical urban consumer.

a. Lipstick index   b. Cost-of-living index

c. Hedonic price index   d. CPI

27.   A _____ is a measure of the average price of consumer goods and services purchased by households. A _____ measures a price change for a constant market basket of goods and services from one period to the next within the same area (city, region, or nation.) It is a price index determined by measuring the price of a standard group of goods meant to represent the typical market basket of a typical urban consumer.

a. CPI   b. Cost-of-living index

c. Lipstick index   d. Consumer Price Index

28.   A _____ is a normalized average (typically a weighted average) of prices for a given class of goods or services in a given region, during a given interval of time. It is a statistic designed to help to compare how these prices, taken as a whole, differ between time periods or geographical locations.

Price indices have several potential uses.

a. Two-part tariff   b. Transactional Net Margin Method

c. Product sabotage   d. Price Index

29.   An _____ is a tax based on the value of real estate or personal property. It is more common than the opposite, a specific duty, or a tax based on the quantity of an item regardless of price.

An _____ is typically imposed at the time of a transaction), but it may be imposed on an annual basis (real or personal property tax) or in connection with another significant event (inheritance tax, surrendering citizenship, or tariffs.)

a. User charge
c. Ad valorem tax

b. Optimal tax
d. Indirect tax

30.   To tax is to impose a financial charge or other levy upon a taxpayer by a state or the functional equivalent of a state.

_____ are also imposed by many subnational entities. _____ consist of direct tax or indirect tax, and may be paid in money or as its labour equivalent (often but not always unpaid.)

a. 100-year flood
c. 1921 recession

b. 130-30 fund
d. Taxes

31.   In economics, _____ is the ratio of the percent change in one variable to the percent change in another variable. It is a tool for measuring the responsiveness of a function to changes in parameters in a relative way. Commonly analyzed are _____ of substitution, price and wealth.

a. Elasticity of demand
c. ACCRA Cost of Living Index

b. ACEA agreement
d. Elasticity

32.   Price _____ is defined as the measure of responsiveness in the quantity demanded for a commodity as a result of change in price of the same commodity. It is a measure of how consumers react to a change in price. In other words, it is percentage change in quantity demanded by the percentage change in price of the same commodity.

a. Elasticity
c. Elasticity of demand

b. ACEA agreement
d. ACCRA Cost of Living Index

33.   In economics, the _____ is defined as a numerical measure of the responsiveness of the quantity supplied of product (A) to a change in price of product (A) alone. It is the measure of the way quantity supplied reacts to a change in price.

For example, if, in response to a 10% rise in the price of a good, the quantity supplied increases by 20%, the _____ would be 20%/10% = 2.

a. Demand shaping
c. Passive income

b. Price elasticity of supply
d. Hedonimetry

1. In economics, _____ is the ability of a firm to alter the market price of a good or service. A firm with _____ can raise prices without losing all customers to competitors.

When a firm has _____ it faces a downward-sloping demand curve.

a. Market power

b. Price makers

c. Revenue-cap regulation

d. Pacman conjecture

2. In economics, a _____ exists when a specific individual or enterprise has sufficient control over a particular product or service to determine significantly the terms on which other individuals shall have access to it. Monopolies are thus characterized by a lack of economic competition for the good or service that they provide and a lack of viable substitute goods. The verb 'monopolize' refers to the process by which a firm gains persistently greater market share than what is expected under perfect competition.

a. Monopoly

b. 1921 recession

c. 100-year flood

d. 130-30 fund

3. In economics, a _____ 'purchase') is a market form in which only one buyer faces many sellers. It is an example of imperfect competition, similar to a monopoly, in which only one seller faces many buyers. As the only purchaser of a good or service, the 'monopsonist' may dictate terms to its suppliers in the same manner that a monopolist controls the market for its buyers.

a. 1921 recession

b. 100-year flood

c. 130-30 fund

d. Monopsony

4. In economics, a _____ occurs when, due to the economies of scale of a particular industry, the maximum efficiency of production and distribution is realized through a single supplier.

Natural monopolies arise where the largest supplier in an industry, often the first supplier in a market, has an overwhelming cost advantage over other actual or potential competitors. This tends to be the case in industries where capital costs predominate, creating economies of scale which are large in relation to the size of the market, and hence high barriers to entry; examples include water services and electricity.

a. Collective goods

b. Privatizing profits and socializing losses

c. Natural Monopoly

d. Common-pool resource

5. In microeconomics, _____ is the extra revenue that an additional unit of product will bring. It is the additional income from selling one more unit of a good; sometimes equal to price. It can also be described as the change in total revenue/change in number of units sold.

a. Reservation price

b. Market demand schedule

c. Long term

d. Marginal revenue

6. In economics, _____ is the process by which a firm determines the price and output level that returns the greatest profit. There are several approaches to this problem. The total revenue--total cost method relies on the fact that profit equals revenue minus cost, and the marginal revenue--marginal cost method is based on the fact that total profit in a perfectly competitive market reaches its maximum point where marginal revenue equals marginal cost.

a. Profit margin

b. Profit maximization

c. 100-year flood

d. Normal profit

7. _____ is one of the four Ps of the marketing mix. The other three aspects are product, promotion, and place. It is also a key variable in microeconomic price allocation theory.

    a. Premium pricing   b. Point of total assumption

    c. Guaranteed Maximum Price   d. Pricing

8. In economics, _____ is the ratio of the percent change in one variable to the percent change in another variable. It is a tool for measuring the responsiveness of a function to changes in parameters in a relative way. Commonly analyzed are _____ of substitution, price and wealth.

    a. Elasticity of demand   b. Elasticity

    c. ACCRA Cost of Living Index   d. ACEA agreement

9. Price _____ is defined as the measure of responsiveness in the quantity demanded for a commodity as a result of change in price of the same commodity. It is a measure of how consumers react to a change in price. In other words, it is percentage change in quantity demanded by the percentage change in price of the same commodity.

    a. ACEA agreement   b. Elasticity of demand

    c. ACCRA Cost of Living Index   d. Elasticity

10. Economics:

- _____, the desire to own something and the ability to pay for it
- _____ curve, a graphic representation of a _____ schedule
- _____ deposit, the money in checking accounts
- _____ pull theory, the theory that inflation occurs when _____ for goods and services exceeds existing supplies
- _____ schedule, a table that lists the quantity of a good a person will buy it each different price
- _____ side economics, the school of economics at believes government spending and tax cuts open economy by raising _____

    a. Variability   b. Production

    c. McKesson ' Robbins scandal   d. Demand

11. _____ is the observation that people often do and believe things because many other people do and believe the same things. The effect is often pejoratively called herding instinct, particularly when applied to adolescents. People tend to follow the crowd without examining the merits of a particular thing.

    a. Halo effect   b. Hyperbolic discounting

    c. Bandwagon effect   d. Sunk costs

12. In economic models, the _____ time frame assumes no fixed factors of production. Firms can enter or leave the marketplace, and the cost (and availability) of land, labor, raw materials, and capital goods can be assumed to vary. In contrast, in the short-run time frame, certain factors are assumed to be fixed, because there is not sufficient time for them to change.

    a. Long-run   b. Price/performance ratio

    c. Diseconomies of scale   d. Productivity world

13. To _____ is to impose a financial charge or other levy upon a taxpayer by a state or the functional equivalent of a state.

_____es are also imposed by many subnational entities. _____es consist of direct _____ or indirect _____, and may be paid in money or as its labour equivalent (often but not always unpaid.)

a. 130-30 fund   b. 100-year flood
c. 1921 recession   d. Tax

14. A _____ is a price discrimination technique in which the price of a product or service is composed of two parts - a lump-sum fee as well as a per-unit charge. In general, price discrimination techniques only occur in partially or fully monopolistic markets. It is designed to enable the firm to capture more consumer surplus than it otherwise would in a non-discriminating pricing environment.

a. Penetration pricing   b. Price floor
c. Big ticket item   d. Two-part tariff

15. A _____ is a duty imposed on goods when they are moved across a political boundary. They are usually associated with protectionism, the economic policy of restraining trade between nations. For political reasons, _____s are usually imposed on imported goods, although they may also be imposed on exported goods.

a. 100-year flood   b. Tariff
c. 1921 recession   d. 130-30 fund

16. The _____ describes a firm's market power. It is defined by:

$$L = \frac{P - MC}{P}$$

where P is the market price set by the firm and MC is the firm's marginal cost. The index ranges from a high of 1 to a low of 0, with higher numbers implying greater market power.

a. Two-part tariff   b. Break even analysis
c. Discounts and allowances   d. Lerner Index

17. _____ refers to the pricing of contributions (assets, tangible and intangible, services, and funds) transferred within an organization. For example, goods from the production division may be sold to the marketing division, or goods from a parent company may be sold to a foreign subsidiary. Since the prices are set within an organization (i.e. controlled), the typical market mechanisms that establish prices for such transactions between third parties may not apply.

a. Two-part tariff   b. Rational pricing
c. Transfer Pricing   d. San Francisco congestion pricing

18. The Organization of the Petroleum Exporting Countries is a cartel of twelve countries made up of Algeria, Angola, Ecuador, Iran, Iraq, Kuwait, Libya, Nigeria, Qatar, Saudi Arabia, the United Arab Emirates, and Venezuela. The cartel has maintained its headquarters in Vienna since 1965, and hosts regular meetings among the oil ministers of its Member Countries. Indonesia withdrew its membership in _____ in 2008 after it became a net importer of oil, but stated it would likely return if it became a net exporter in the world.

a. ACEA agreement

b. AD-IA Model

c. ACCRA Cost of Living Index

d. OPEC

19.   In economics and especially in the theory of competition, _____ are obstacles in the path of a firm that make it difficult to enter a given market.

_____ are the source of a firm's pricing power - the ability of a firm to raise prices without losing all its customers.

The term refers to hindrances that an individual may face while trying to gain entrance into a profession or trade.

a. Group boycott

b. Social dumping

c. Limit price

d. Barriers to entry

20.   In economics, the _____ of an industry is used as an indicator of the relative size of firms in relation to the industry as a whole. It is calculated as the sum of the percent market share of the top n industries. This may also assist in determining the market structure of the industry.

a. Pacman conjecture

b. Concentration ratio

c. Quasi-rent

d. Monopolization

21.   _____, in microeconomics, are the cost advantages that a business obtains due to expansion. They are factors that cause a producere;s average cost per unit to fall as scale is increased. _____ is a long run concept and refers to reductions in unit cost as the size of a facility, or scale, increases.

a. Underinvestment employment relationship

b. Economies of scale

c. Isoquant

d. Economic production quantity

22.   A _____ is a set of exclusive rights granted by a state to an inventor or his assignee for a limited period of time in exchange for a disclosure of an invention.

The procedure for granting _____s, the requirements placed on the _____ee and the extent of the exclusive rights vary widely between countries according to national laws and international agreements. Typically, however, a _____ application must include one or more claims defining the invention which must be new, inventive, and useful or industrially applicable.

a. Bank regulation

b. Long service leave

c. Bona fide occupational qualification

d. Patent

23.   A _____ is an expression that compares quantities relative to each other. The most common examples involve two quantities, but any number of quantities can be compared. _____s are represented mathematically by separating each quantity with a colon, for example the _____ 2:3, which is read as the _____ 'two to three'.

a. Y-intercept

b. 130-30 fund

c. Ratio

d. 100-year flood

24.   In economics, a _____ is a loss of economic efficiency that can occur when equilibrium for a good or service is not Pareto optimal. In other words, either people who would have more marginal benefit than marginal cost are not buying the good or service, or people who would have more marginal cost than marginal benefit are buying the product.

Causes of _____ can include monopoly pricing, externalities, taxes or subsidies, and binding price ceilings or floors.

a. Contract curve   b. Deadweight loss
c. Distributive efficiency   d. Leapfrogging

25.   In economics _____ is defined as the sum of private and external costs. Economic theorists ascribe individual decision-making to a calculation costs and benefits. Rational choice theory assumes that individuals only consider their own private costs when making decisions, not the costs that may be borne by others.
a. Cost-Volume-Profit Analysis   b. Psychic cost
c. Social cost   d. Khozraschyot

26.   _____ was a survey conducted by the U.S. Department of Justice to gauge the prevalence of alcohol and illegal drug use among prior arrestees. It was a reformulation of the prior Drug Use Forecasting (DUF) program, focused on five drugs in particular: cocaine, marijuana, methamphetamine, opiates, and PCP.

Participants were randomly selected from arrest records in major metropolitan areas; because no personally identifying information is taken from each record chosen, the resulting data can be correlated to arrest rates, but not to the total population of persons charged.

a. Arrestee Drug Abuse Monitoring   b. ACEA agreement
c. AD-IA Model   d. ACCRA Cost of Living Index

27.   Economic _____ is defined as an excess distribution to any factor in a production process above that which is required to induce the factor into the process or any excess above that which is necessary to keep the factor in its current use..

Classical Factor _____ is primarily concerned with the fee paid for the use of fixed (e.g. natural) resources. The classical definition is expressed as any excess payment above that required to induce or provide for production.

a. 1921 recession   b. 130-30 fund
c. 100-year flood   d. Rent

28.   In economics, _____ occurs when an individual, organization or firm seeks to make money through economic rent.

_____ generally implies the extraction of uncompensated value from others without making any contribution to productivity, such as by gaining control of land and other pre-existing natural resources, or by imposing burdensome regulations or other government decisions that may affect consumers or businesses. While there may be few people in modern industrialized countries who do not gain something, directly or indirectly, through some form or another of _____, Rent seeking in the aggregate imposes substantial losses on society.

a. Rent seeking

b. Good governance

c. 130-30 fund

d. 100-year flood

29. _____ in economics and business is the result of an exchange and from that trade we assign a numerical monetary value to a good, service or asset. If Alice trades Bob 4 apples for an orange, the _____ of an orange is 4 apples. Inversely, the _____ of an apple is 1/4 oranges.

a. Price book

b. Price war

c. Premium pricing

d. Price

30. _____ is a system for setting the prices charged by regulated monopolies. The central idea is that monopoly firms should be required to charge the price that would prevail in a competitive market, which is equal to efficient costs of production plus a market-determined rate of return on capital.

_____ has been criticized because it encourages cost-padding, and because, if the allowable rate is set too high, it encourages the adoption of an inefficiently high capital-labor ratio.

a. Complementary monopoly

b. Market concentration

c. Revenue-cap regulation

d. Rate-of-return regulation

31. An _____ is a market form in which the number of buyers is small while the number of sellers in theory could be large. This typically happens in market for inputs where a small number of firms are competing to obtain factors of production. It contrasts with an oligopoly, where there are many buyers but just a few sellers.

a. ACEA agreement

b. Oligopsony

c. Oligopoly

d. ACCRA Cost of Living Index

32. _____ is the a method of technical and economic research of the systems for purpose to optimize a parity between system's consumer functions or properties and expenses to achieve those functions or properties.

This methodology for continuous perfection of production, industrial technologies, organizational structures was developed by Juryj Sobolev in 1948 at the 'Perm telephone factory'

- 1948 Juryj Sobolev - the first success in application of a method analysis at the 'Perm telephone factory' .
- 1949 - the first application for the invention as result of use of the new method.

Today in economically developed countries practically each enterprise or the company use methodology of the kind of functional-cost analysis as a practice of the quality management, most full satisfying to principles of standards of series ISO 9000.

- Interest of consumer not in products itself, but the advantage which it will receive from its usage.
- The consumer aspires to reduce his expenses
- Functions needed by consumer can be executed in the various ways, and, hence, with various efficiency and expenses. Among possible alternatives of realization of functions exist such in which the parity of quality and the price is the optimal for the consumer.

The goal of _____ is achievement of the highest consumer satisfaction of production at simultaneous decrease in all kinds of industrial expenses Classical _____ has three English synonyms - Value Engineering, Value Management, Value Analysis.

a. Willingness to pay

b. Function cost analysis

c. Staple financing

d. Monopoly wage

33.   In economics, a monopsony 'purchase') is a market form in which only one buyer faces many sellers. It is an example of imperfect competition, similar to a monopoly, in which only one seller faces many buyers. As the only purchaser of a good or service, the '_____' may dictate terms to its suppliers in the same manner that a monopolist controls the market for its buyers.

a. 100-year flood

b. 1921 recession

c. 130-30 fund

d. Monopsonist

34.   In economics, the _____ is defined as a numerical measure of the responsiveness of the quantity supplied of product (A) to a change in price of product (A) alone. It is the measure of the way quantity supplied reacts to a change in price.

For example, if, in response to a 10% rise in the price of a good, the quantity supplied increases by 20%, the _____ would be 20%/10% = 2.

a. Demand shaping

b. Hedonimetry

c. Passive income

d. Price elasticity of supply

35.   _____ refers to the state of not requiring any outside aid, support for survival; it is therefore a type of personal or collective autonomy. On a large scale, a totally self-sufficient economy that does not trade with the outside world is called an autarky.

The term _____ is usually applied to varieties of sustainable living in which nothing is consumed outside of what is produced by the self-sufficient individuals.

a. Sustainability science

b. Sustainable forest management

c. Global Reporting Initiative

d. Self-sufficiency

36.   Competition law, known in the United States as _____ law, has three main elements:

- prohibiting agreements or practices that restrict free trading and competition between business entities. This includes in particular the repression of cartels.
- banning abusive behaviour by a firm dominating a market, or anti-competitive practices that tend to lead to such a dominant position. Practices controlled in this way may include predatory pricing, tying, price gouging, refusal to deal, and many others.
- supervising the mergers and acquisitions of large corporations, including some joint ventures. Transactions that are considered to threaten the competitive process can be prohibited altogether, or approved subject to 'remedies' such as an obligation to divest part of the merged business or to offer licences or access to facilities to enable other businesses to continue competing.

The substance and practice of competition law varies from jurisdiction to jurisdiction. Protecting the interests of consumers (consumer welfare) and ensuring that entrepreneurs have an opportunity to compete in the market economy are often treated as important objectives. Competition law is closely connected with law on deregulation of access to markets, state aids and subsidies, the privatisation of state owned assets and the establishment of independent sector regulators. In recent decades, competition law has been viewed as a way to provide better public services.

a. Intellectual property law   b. Anti-Inflation Act
c. United Kingdom competition law   d. Antitrust

37.   _____, known in the United States as antitrust law, has three main elements:

- prohibiting agreements or practices that restrict free trading and competition between business entities. This includes in particular the repression of cartels.
- banning abusive behaviour by a firm dominating a market, or anti-competitive practices that tend to lead to such a dominant position. Practices controlled in this way may include predatory pricing, tying, price gouging, refusal to deal, and many others.
- supervising the mergers and acquisitions of large corporations, including some joint ventures. Transactions that are considered to threaten the competitive process can be prohibited altogether, or approved subject to 'remedies' such as an obligation to divest part of the merged business or to offer licences or access to facilities to enable other businesses to continue competing.

The substance and practice of _____ varies from jurisdiction to jurisdiction. Protecting the interests of consumers (consumer welfare) and ensuring that entrepreneurs have an opportunity to compete in the market economy are often treated as important objectives. _____ is closely connected with law on deregulation of access to markets, state aids and subsidies, the privatisation of state owned assets and the establishment of independent sector regulators. In recent decades, _____ has been viewed as a way to provide better public services.

a. Competition law   b. Fee simple
c. Due diligence   d. Hostile work environment

38. The _____ is an independent agency of the United States government, established in 1914 by the _____ Act. Its principal mission is the promotion of 'consumer protection' and the elimination and prevention of what regulators perceive to be harmfully 'anti-competitive' business practices, such as coercive monopoly.

The _____ Act was one of President Wilson's major acts against trusts.

a. 100-year flood   b. 130-30 fund
c. 1921 recession   d. Federal Trade Commission

39. The _____ of 1914 (15 U.S.C §§ 41-58, as amended) established the Federal Trade Commission (FTC), a bipartisan body of five members appointed by the President of the United States for seven year terms. This Commission was authorized to issue Cease and Desist orders to large corporations to curb unfair trade practices. This Act also gave more flexibility to the US congress for judicial matters.

a. Buydown   b. Competition law theory
c. Federal Trade Commission Act   d. Minimum wage law

40. _____ is the practice of selling a product or service at a very low price, intending to drive competitors out of the market, or create barriers to entry for potential new competitors. If competitors or potential competitors cannot sustain equal or lower prices without losing money, they go out of business or choose not to enter the business. The predatory merchant then has fewer competitors or is even a de facto monopoly, and can then raise prices above what the market would otherwise bear.

a. Third line forcing   b. Restraint of trade
c. Group boycott   d. Predatory pricing

41. _____ refers to the procedure of reviewing mergers and acquisitions under antitrust / competition law. Over 60 nations worldwide have adopted a regime providing for _____.

_____ regimes are adopted to prevent anti-competitive consequences of concentrations (as mergers/takeovers are also known.)

a. Merger Control   b. 130-30 fund
c. 1921 recession   d. 100-year flood

42. The _____ is responsible for enforcing the antitrust laws of the United States. It shares jurisdiction over civil antitrust cases with the Federal Trade Commission (FTC) and often works jointly with the FTC to provide regulatory guidance to businesses. However, the Antitrust Division also has the power to file criminal cases against willful violators of the antitrust laws.

a. Antitrust   b. United States Department of Justice Antitrust Division
c. Intellectual property law   d. Ease of Doing Business Index

43. The _____ consists of a number of economic theories which describe the nature of the firm, company including its existence, its behaviour, and its relationship with the market.

In simplified terms, the _____ aims to answer these questions:

1. Existence - why do firms emerge, why are not all transactions in the economy mediated over the market?
2. Boundaries - why the boundary between firms and the market is located exactly there? Which transactions are performed internally and which are negotiated on the market?
3. Organization - why are firms structured in such specific way? What is the interplay of formal and informal relationships?

Despite looking simple, these questions are not answered by the established economic theory, which usually views firms as given, and treats them as black boxes without any internal structure.

The First World War period saw a change of emphasis in economic theory away from industry-level analysis which mainly included analysing markets to analysis at the level of the firm, as it became increasingly clear that perfect competition was no longer an adequate model of how firms behaved. Economic theory till then had focussed on trying to understand markets alone and there had been little study on understanding why firms or organisations exist.

a. Khazzoom-Brookes postulate

b. Theory of the firm

c. Policy Ineffectiveness Proposition

d. Technology gap

1. The _____ consists of a number of economic theories which describe the nature of the firm, company including its existence, its behaviour, and its relationship with the market.

In simplified terms, the _____ aims to answer these questions:

1. Existence - why do firms emerge, why are not all transactions in the economy mediated over the market?
2. Boundaries - why the boundary between firms and the market is located exactly there? Which transactions are performed internally and which are negotiated on the market?
3. Organization - why are firms structured in such specific way? What is the interplay of formal and informal relationships?

Despite looking simple, these questions are not answered by the established economic theory, which usually views firms as given, and treats them as black boxes without any internal structure.

The First World War period saw a change of emphasis in economic theory away from industry-level analysis which mainly included analysing markets to analysis at the level of the firm, as it became increasingly clear that perfect competition was no longer an adequate model of how firms behaved. Economic theory till then had focussed on trying to understand markets alone and there had been little study on understanding why firms or organisations exist.

a. Khazzoom-Brookes postulate   b. Policy Ineffectiveness Proposition
c. Technology gap   d. Theory of the firm

2. In economics, _____ is the ability of a firm to alter the market price of a good or service. A firm with _____ can raise prices without losing all customers to competitors.

When a firm has _____ it faces a downward-sloping demand curve.

a. Revenue-cap regulation   b. Price makers
c. Pacman conjecture   d. Market power

3. _____ in economics and business is the result of an exchange and from that trade we assign a numerical monetary value to a good, service or asset. If Alice trades Bob 4 apples for an orange, the _____ of an orange is 4 apples. Inversely, the _____ of an apple is 1/4 oranges.

a. Price book   b. Premium pricing
c. Price war   d. Price

4. _____ is one of the four Ps of the marketing mix. The other three aspects are product, promotion, and place. It is also a key variable in microeconomic price allocation theory.

a. Premium pricing   b. Pricing
c. Point of total assumption   d. Guaranteed Maximum Price

5. A _____ is a price discrimination technique in which the price of a product or service is composed of two parts - a lump-sum fee as well as a per-unit charge. In general, price discrimination techniques only occur in partially or fully monopolistic markets. It is designed to enable the firm to capture more consumer surplus than it otherwise would in a non-discriminating pricing environment.

a. Penetration pricing

c. Two-part tariff

b. Price floor

d. Big ticket item

6.   A _____ is a duty imposed on goods when they are moved across a political boundary. They are usually associated with protectionism, the economic policy of restraining trade between nations. For political reasons, _____s are usually imposed on imported goods, although they may also be imposed on exported goods.

a. 130-30 fund

c. 1921 recession

b. 100-year flood

d. Tariff

7.   _____ is a broad label that refers to any individuals or households that use goods and services generated within the economy. The concept of a _____ is used in different contexts, so that the usage and significance of the term may vary.

Typically when business people and economists talk of _____s they are talking about person as _____, an aggregated commodity item with little individuality other than that expressed in the buy/not-buy decision.

a. 130-30 fund

c. 100-year flood

b. 1921 recession

d. Consumer

8.   The term surplus is used in economics for several related quantities. The _____ is the amount that consumers benefit by being able to purchase a product for a price that is less than they would be willing to pay. The producer surplus is the amount that producers benefit by selling at a market price mechanism that is higher than they would be willing to sell for.

a. Marginal rate of technical substitution

c. Necessity good

b. Microeconomic reform

d. Consumer surplus

9.   _____ exists when sales of identical goods or services are transacted at different prices from the same provider. In a theoretical market with perfect information, no transaction costs or prohibition on secondary exchange (or re-selling) to prevent arbitrage, _____ can only be a feature of monopoly and oligopoly markets, where market power can be exercised. Otherwise, the moment the seller tries to sell the same good at different prices, the buyer at the lower price can arbitrage by selling to the consumer buying at the higher price but with a tiny discount.

a. Lerner Index

c. Transfer pricing

b. Loss leader

d. Price discrimination

10.   In microeconomics, the reservation (or reserve) price is the maximum price a buyer is willing to pay for a good or service; or, conversely, the minimum price at which a seller is willing to sell a good or service. _____s are commonly used in auctions.

_____s vary for the buyer according to their disposable income, their desire for the good, and the prices of, and their information about substitute goods.

a. Mohring effect

c. Returns to scale

b. Producer surplus

d. Reservation price

11. _____ is the study of when, why, how, where and what people do or do not buy products. It blends elements from psychology, sociology,social psychology, anthropology and economics. It attempts to understand the buyer decision making process, both individually and in groups.

   a. Consumer behavior   b. Consumption smoothing

   c. Situational theory of publics   d. Shopping Neutral

12. _____s is the social science that studies the production, distribution, and consumption of goods and services. The term _____s comes from the Ancient Greek οἰκονομία from οἶκος (oikos, 'house') + νόμος (nomos, 'custom' or 'law'), hence 'rules of the house(hold)'. Current _____ models developed out of the broader field of political economy in the late 19th century, owing to a desire to use an empirical approach more akin to the physical sciences.

   a. Economic   b. Opportunity cost

   c. Inflation   d. Energy economics

13. _____ is a specific term used in companies' financial reporting from the company-whole point of view. Because that use excludes the effects of changing ownership interest, an economic measure of _____ is necessary for financial analysis from the shareholders' point of view

_____ is defined by the Financial Accounting Standards Board, or FASB, as e;the change in equity [net assets] of a business enterprise during a period from transactions and other events and circumstances from nonowner sources. It includes all changes in equity during a period except those resulting from investments by owners and distributions to owners.e;

_____ is the sum of net income and other items that must bypass the income statement because they have not been realized, including items like an unrealized holding gain or loss from available for sale securities and foreign currency translation gains or losses.

   a. Comprehensive income   b. Net national income

   c. Real income   d. Windfall gain

14. _____ is a pricing technique applied to public goods, which is a particular case of a Lindahl equilibrium. Instead of different demands for the same public good, we consider the demands for a public good in different periods of the day, month or year, then finding the optimal capacity (quantity supplied) and, afterwards, the optimal peak-load prices.

This has particular applications in public goods such as public urban transportation, where day demand (peak period) is usually much higher than night demand (off-peak period.)

   a. Fiscal imbalance   b. Demand management

   c. Cobra effect   d. Peak-load pricing

15. _____ is used to refer to a number of related concepts. It is the using resources in such a way as to maximize the production of goods and services. A system can be called economically efficient if:

- No one can be made better off without making someone else worse off.
- More output cannot be obtained without increasing the amount of inputs.
- Production proceeds at the lowest possible per-unit cost.

These definitions of efficiency are not equivalent, but they are all encompassed by the idea that nothing more can be achieved given the resources available.

An economic system is more efficient if it can provide more goods and services for society without using more resources.

a. ACEA agreement

b. ACCRA Cost of Living Index

c. Efficient contract theory

d. Economic efficiency

16. In economics, and cost accounting, _____ describes the total economic cost of production and is made up of variable costs, which vary according to the quantity of a good produced and include inputs such as labor and raw materials, plus fixed costs, which are independent of the quantity of a good produced and include inputs (capital) that cannot be varied in the short term, such as buildings and machinery. _____ in economics includes the total opportunity cost of each factor of production in addition to fixed and variable costs.

The rate at which _____ changes as the amount produced changes is called marginal cost.

a. 1921 recession

b. 100-year flood

c. 130-30 fund

d. Total cost

17. Under the system of feudalism, a _____, fief, feud, feoff often consisted of inheritable lands or revenue-producing property granted by a liege lord, generally to a vassal, in return for a form of allegiance, originally to give him the means to fulfill his military duties when called upon. However anything of value could be held in fief, such as an office, a right of exploitation (e.g., hunting, fishing) or any other type of revenue, rather than the land it comes from.

Originally, the feudal institution of vassalage did not imply the giving or receiving of landholdings (which were granted only as a reward for loyalty), but by the eighth century the giving of a landholding was becoming standard.

a. 130-30 fund

b. 1921 recession

c. 100-year flood

d. Fiefdom

18. _____ is a generic term that refers to the notion of comparing the price of an asset to the market value of similar assets. In the field of securities investment, the idea has led to important practical tools, which could presumably spot pricing anomalies. These tools have subsequently become instrumental in enabling analysts and investors to make vital decisions on asset allocation.

a. Growth investing

b. Relative valuation

c. Shadow stock

d. Buy side

19. A _____ is a place of residence or refuge and comfort. It is usually a place in which an individual or a family can rest and be able to store personal property. Most modern-day households contain sanitary facilities and a means of preparing food.

a. 1921 recession

b. 100-year flood

c. 130-30 fund

d. Home

20.   In economics, _____ is the ratio of the percent change in one variable to the percent change in another variable. It is a tool for measuring the responsiveness of a function to changes in parameters in a relative way. Commonly analyzed are _____ of substitution, price and wealth.
  a. ACCRA Cost of Living Index   b. ACEA agreement
  c. Elasticity   d. Elasticity of demand

21.   Price _____ is defined as the measure of responsiveness in the quantity demanded for a commodity as a result of change in price of the same commodity. It is a measure of how consumers react to a change in price. In other words, it is percentage change in quantity demanded by the percentage change in price of the same commodity.
  a. ACEA agreement   b. Elasticity
  c. ACCRA Cost of Living Index   d. Elasticity of demand

22.   Economics:

  - _____,the desire to own something and the ability to pay for it
  - _____ curve,a graphic representation of a _____ schedule
  - _____ deposit, the money in checking accounts
  - _____ pull theory,the theory that inflation occurs when _____ for goods and services exceeds existing supplies
  - _____ schedule,a table that lists the quantity of a good a person will buy it each different price
  - _____ side economics,the school of economics at believes government spending and tax cuts open economy by raising _____

  a. Variability   b. Demand
  c. McKesson ' Robbins scandal   d. Production

23.   A _____ is an expression that compares quantities relative to each other. The most common examples involve two quantities, but any number of quantities can be compared. _____s are represented mathematically by separating each quantity with a colon, for example the _____ 2:3, which is read as the _____ 'two to three'.
  a. 100-year flood   b. Y-intercept
  c. 130-30 fund   d. Ratio

24. A _____ is:

- Rewrite _____, in generative grammar and computer science
- Standardization, a formal and widely-accepted statement, fact, definition, or qualification
- Operation, a determinate _____ for performing a mathematical operation and obtaining a certain result (Mathematics, Logic)
    - ○ Unary operation
    - ○ Binary operation
- _____ of inference, a function from sets of formulae to formulae (Mathematics, Logic)
- _____ of thumb, principle with broad application that is not intended to be strictly accurate or reliable for every situation. Also often simply referred to as a _____
- Moral, an atomic element of a moral code for guiding choices in human behavior
- Heuristic, a quantized '_____' which shows a tendency or probability for successful function
- A regulation, as in sports
- A Production _____, as in computer science
- Procedural law, a _____ set governing the application of laws to cases
    - ○ A law, which may informally be called a '_____'
    - ○ A court ruling, a decision by a court
- In the U.S. Government, a regulation mandated by Congress, but written or expanded upon by the Executive Branch.
- Norm (sociology), an informal but widely accepted _____, concept, truth, definition, or qualification (social norms, legal norms, coding norms)
- Norm (philosophy), a kind of sentence or a reason to act, feel or believe
- 'Rulership' is the concept of governance by a government:
    - ○ Military _____, governance by a military body
    - ○ Monastic _____, a collection of precepts that guides the life of monks or nuns in a religious order where the superior holds the place of Christ
- Slide _____

- '_____,' a song by Ayumi Hamasaki
- '_____,' a song by rapper Nas
- '_____s,' an album by the band The Whitest Boy Alive
- _____s: Pyaar Ka Superhit Formula, a 2003 Bollywood film
- ruler, an instrument for measuring lengths
- _____, a component of an astrolabe, circumferator or similar instrument
- The _____s, a bestselling self-help book
- _____ Project (Run Up-to-date Linux Everywhere), a project that aims to use up-to-date Linux software on old PCs
- _____ engine, a software system that helps managing business _____s
- Ja _____, a hip hop artist
    - ○ R.U.L.E., a 2005 greatest hits album by rapper Ja _____
- '_____s,' a KMFDM song

a. Demand

b. Procter ' Gamble

c. Technocracy

d. Rule

25. In economics, _____ is the process by which a firm determines the price and output level that returns the greatest profit. There are several approaches to this problem. The total revenue--total cost method relies on the fact that profit equals revenue minus cost, and the marginal revenue--marginal cost method is based on the fact that total profit in a perfectly competitive market reaches its maximum point where marginal revenue equals marginal cost.

a. Normal profit   b. 100-year flood
c. Profit margin   d. Profit maximization

26. _____ refers to the pricing of contributions (assets, tangible and intangible, services, and funds) transferred within an organization. For example, goods from the production division may be sold to the marketing division, or goods from a parent company may be sold to a foreign subsidiary. Since the prices are set within an organization (i.e. controlled), the typical market mechanisms that establish prices for such transactions between third parties may not apply.

a. San Francisco congestion pricing   b. Transfer pricing
c. Two-part tariff   d. Rational pricing

1. _____ is a common market structure where many competing producers sell products that are differentiated from one another (ie. the products are substitutes, but are not exactly alike.) Many markets are monopolistically competitive, common examples include the markets for restaurants, cereal, clothing, shoes and service industries in large cities.

   a. Perfect competition   b. Monopolistic competition

   c. Financial crisis   d. Mathematical economics

2. An _____ is a market form in which a market or industry is dominated by a small number of sellers (oligopolists.) Because there are few participants in this type of market, each oligopolist is aware of the actions of the others. The decisions of one firm influence, and are influenced by, the decisions of other firms.

   a. ACEA agreement   b. Oligopoly

   c. ACCRA Cost of Living Index   d. Oligopsony

3. A _____ is a counterfeit agreement among industries. It is an informal organization of producers that agree to coordinate prices and production. _____s usually occur in an oligopolistic industry, where there is a small number of sellers and usually involve homogeneous products.

   a. Cartel   b. Shanzhai

   c. 100-year flood   d. Shill

4. The Organization of the Petroleum Exporting Countries is a cartel of twelve countries made up of Algeria, Angola, Ecuador, Iran, Iraq, Kuwait, Libya, Nigeria, Qatar, Saudi Arabia, the United Arab Emirates, and Venezuela. The cartel has maintained its headquarters in Vienna since 1965, and hosts regular meetings among the oil ministers of its Member Countries. Indonesia withdrew its membership in _____ in 2008 after it became a net importer of oil, but stated it would likely return if it became a net exporter in the world.

   a. AD-IA Model   b. ACEA agreement

   c. ACCRA Cost of Living Index   d. OPEC

5. Procter is a surname, and may also refer to:

   - Bryan Waller Procter (pseud. Barry Cornwall), English poet
   - Goodwin Procter, American law firm
   - _____, consumer products multinational

   a. Procter ' Gamble   b. Drawdown

   c. Tightness   d. Bucket shop

6. _____s is the social science that studies the production, distribution, and consumption of goods and services. The term _____s comes from the Ancient Greek οá¼°κονομῖα from οá¼¶κος (oikos, 'house') + νῐΌμος (nomos, 'custom' or 'law'), hence 'rules of the house(hold)'. Current _____ models developed out of the broader field of political economy in the late 19th century, owing to a desire to use an empirical approach more akin to the physical sciences.

   a. Opportunity cost   b. Energy economics

   c. Economic   d. Inflation

7. _____ is used to refer to a number of related concepts. It is the using resources in such a way as to maximize the production of goods and services. A system can be called economically efficient if:

- No one can be made better off without making someone else worse off.
- More output cannot be obtained without increasing the amount of inputs.
- Production proceeds at the lowest possible per-unit cost.

These definitions of efficiency are not equivalent, but they are all encompassed by the idea that nothing more can be achieved given the resources available.

An economic system is more efficient if it can provide more goods and services for society without using more resources.

a. ACEA agreement   b. ACCRA Cost of Living Index
c. Efficient contract theory   d. Economic efficiency

8. In economics, _____ is the difference between a company's total revenue and its opportunity costs. It is the increase in wealth that an investor has from making an investment, taking into consideration all costs associated with that investment including the opportunity cost of capital.

Profit is the factor income of the entrepreneur.

a. Operating profit   b. ACCRA Cost of Living Index
c. Accounting profit   d. Economic profit

9. In economics, _____ is the process by which a firm determines the price and output level that returns the greatest profit. There are several approaches to this problem. The total revenue--total cost method relies on the fact that profit equals revenue minus cost, and the marginal revenue--marginal cost method is based on the fact that total profit in a perfectly competitive market reaches its maximum point where marginal revenue equals marginal cost.

a. Profit maximization   b. Normal profit
c. Profit margin   d. 100-year flood

10. _____ is the difference between price and the costs of bringing to market whatever it is that is accounted as an enterprise (whether by harvest, extraction, manufacture, or purchase) in terms of the component costs of delivered goods and/or services and any operating or other expenses.

A key difficulty in measuring profit is in defining costs. Pure economic monetary profits can be zero or negative even in competitive equilibrium when accounted monetized costs exceed monetized price.

a. Accounting profit   b. Operating profit
c. ACCRA Cost of Living Index   d. Economic profit

11.   Competitive market equilibrium is the traditional concept of economic equilibrium, appropriate for the analysis of commodity markets with flexible prices and many traders, and serving as the benchmark of efficiency in economic analysis. It relies crucially on the assumption of a competitive environment where each trader decides upon a quantity that is so small compared to the total quantity traded in the market that their individual transactions have no influence on the prices.Competitive markets are an ideal, a standard that other market structures are evaluated by.

A _____ consists of a vector of prices and an allocation such that given the prices, each trader by maximizing his objective function (profit, preferences) subject to his technological possibilities and resource constraints plans to trade into his part of the proposed allocation, and such that the prices make all net trades compatible with one another ('clear the market') by equating aggregate supply and demand for the commodities which are traded.

a. Market system   b. Product-Market Growth Matrix
c. Partial equilibrium   d. Competitive equilibrium

12.   Economics:

- _____,the desire to own something and the ability to pay for it
- _____ curve,a graphic representation of a _____ schedule
- _____ deposit, the money in checking accounts
- _____ pull theory,the theory that inflation occurs when _____ for goods and services exceeds existing supplies
- _____ schedule,a table that lists the quantity of a good a person will buy it each different price
- _____ side economics,the school of economics at believes government spending and tax cuts open economy by raising _____

a. McKesson ' Robbins scandal   b. Production
c. Variability   d. Demand

13.   In economics, the _____ can be defined as the graph depicting the relationship between the price of a certain commodity, and the amount of it that consumers are willing and able to purchase at that given price. It is a graphic representation of a demand schedule. The _____ for all consumers together follows from the _____ of every individual consumer: the individual demands at each price are added together.
a. Cost curve   b. Kuznets curve
c. Wage curve   d. Demand curve

14.   In economics, the concept of the _____ refers to the decision-making time frame of a firm in which at least one factor of production is fixed. Costs which are fixed in the _____ have no impact on a firms decisions. For example a firm can raise output by increasing the amount of labour through overtime.
a. Productivity model   b. Hicks-neutral technical change
c. Product Pipeline   d. Short-run

15.   In economics, and cost accounting, _____ describes the total economic cost of production and is made up of variable costs, which vary according to the quantity of a good produced and include inputs such as labor and raw materials, plus fixed costs, which are independent of the quantity of a good produced and include inputs (capital) that cannot be varied in the short term, such as buildings and machinery. _____ in economics includes the total opportunity cost of each factor of production in addition to fixed and variable costs.

The rate at which _____ changes as the amount produced changes is called marginal cost.

a. 100-year flood   b. Total cost

c. 1921 recession   d. 130-30 fund

16.   In economics and especially in the theory of competition, _____ are obstacles in the path of a firm that make it difficult to enter a given market.

_____ are the source of a firm's pricing power - the ability of a firm to raise prices without losing all its customers.

The term refers to hindrances that an individual may face while trying to gain entrance into a profession or trade.

a. Barriers to entry   b. Social dumping

c. Limit price   d. Group boycott

17.   In game theory, _____ is a solution concept of a game involving two or more players, in which each player is assumed to know the equilibrium strategies of the other players, and no player has anything to gain by changing only his or her own strategy unilaterally. If each player has chosen a strategy and no player can benefit by changing his or her strategy while the other players keep theirs unchanged, then the current set of strategy choices and the corresponding payoffs constitute a _____.

Stated simply, Amy and Bill are in _____ if Amy is making the best decision she can, taking into account Bill's decision, and Bill is making the best decision he can, taking into account Amy's decision.

a. Proper equilibrium   b. Linear production game

c. Lump of labour   d. Nash equilibrium

18.   _____ is an economic model used to describe an industry structure in which companies compete on the amount of output they will produce, which they decide on independently of each other and at the same time. It is named after Antoine Augustin Cournot (1801-1877) after he observed competition in a spring water duopoly. It has the following features:

- There is more than one firm and all firms produce a homogeneous product, i.e. there is no product differentiation;
- Firms do not cooperate, i.e. there is no collusion;
- Firms have market power, i.e. each firm's output decision affects the good's price;
- The number of firms is fixed;
- Firms compete in quantities, and choose quantities simultaneously;
- The firms are economically rational and act strategically, usually seeking to maximize profit given their competitors' decisions.

An essential assumption of this model is that each firm aims to maximize profits, based on the expectation that its own output decision will not have an effect on the decisions of its rivals. Price is a commonly known decreasing function of total output.

a. 130-30 fund

b. 100-year flood

c. 1921 recession

d. Cournot competition

19.   A true _____ is a specific type of oligopoly where only two producers exist in one market. In reality, this definition is generally used where only two firms have dominant control over a market. In the field of industrial organization, it is the most commonly studied form of oligopoly due to its simplicity.

a. Megacorpstate

b. 130-30 fund

c. 100-year flood

d. Duopoly

20.   _____ is an agreement, usually secretive, which occurs between two or more persons to deceive, mislead or to obtain an objective forbidden by law typically involving fraud or gaining an unfair advantage. It is an agreement among firms to divide the market, set prices kickbacks, or misrepresenting the independence of the relationship between the colluding parties.' All acts effected by _____ are considered void.

a. Collusion

b. Net Book Agreement

c. Dividing territories

d. Bid rigging

21.   _____ in economics and business is the result of an exchange and from that trade we assign a numerical monetary value to a good, service or asset. If Alice trades Bob 4 apples for an orange, the _____ of an orange is 4 apples. Inversely, the _____ of an apple is 1/4 oranges.

a. Price book

b. Price war

c. Premium pricing

d. Price

22.   _____ is one of the four Ps of the marketing mix. The other three aspects are product, promotion, and place. It is also a key variable in microeconomic price allocation theory.

a. Guaranteed Maximum Price

b. Point of total assumption

c. Premium pricing

d. Pricing

23.   The _____ curve theory is an economic theory regarding oligopoly and monopolistic competition. When it was created, the idea fundamentally challenged classical economic tenets such as efficient markets and rapidly-changing prices, ideas that underly basic supply and demand models. _____ was an initial attempt to explain sticky prices.

a. Kinked demand curve

b. Marginal demand

c. Precautionary demand

d. Kinked demand

24.   The _____ theory is an economic theory regarding oligopoly and monopolistic competition. When it was created, the idea fundamentally challenged classical economic tenets such as efficient markets and rapidly-changing prices, ideas that underly basic supply and demand models. Kinked demand was an initial attempt to explain sticky prices.

a. Hicksian demand function

b. Precautionary demand

c. Kinked demand

d. Kinked demand curve

25. _____ is a term applied in many countries to a reference interest rate used by banks. The term originally indicated the rate of interest at which banks lent to favored customers, i.e., those with high credibility, though this is no longer always the case. Some variable interest rates may be expressed as a percentage above or below _____.

   a. Prime rate   b. Capital requirement
   c. Transactional account   d. Repo Rate

26.   Competition law, known in the United States as _____ law, has three main elements:

   - prohibiting agreements or practices that restrict free trading and competition between business entities. This includes in particular the repression of cartels.
   - banning abusive behaviour by a firm dominating a market, or anti-competitive practices that tend to lead to such a dominant position. Practices controlled in this way may include predatory pricing, tying, price gouging, refusal to deal, and many others.
   - supervising the mergers and acquisitions of large corporations, including some joint ventures. Transactions that are considered to threaten the competitive process can be prohibited altogether, or approved subject to 'remedies' such as an obligation to divest part of the merged business or to offer licences or access to facilities to enable other businesses to continue competing.

The substance and practice of competition law varies from jurisdiction to jurisdiction. Protecting the interests of consumers (consumer welfare) and ensuring that entrepreneurs have an opportunity to compete in the market economy are often treated as important objectives. Competition law is closely connected with law on deregulation of access to markets, state aids and subsidies, the privatisation of state owned assets and the establishment of independent sector regulators. In recent decades, competition law has been viewed as a way to provide better public services.

   a. Antitrust   b. Anti-Inflation Act
   c. United Kingdom competition law   d. Intellectual property law

27.   _____, known in the United States as antitrust law, has three main elements:

   - prohibiting agreements or practices that restrict free trading and competition between business entities. This includes in particular the repression of cartels.
   - banning abusive behaviour by a firm dominating a market, or anti-competitive practices that tend to lead to such a dominant position. Practices controlled in this way may include predatory pricing, tying, price gouging, refusal to deal, and many others.
   - supervising the mergers and acquisitions of large corporations, including some joint ventures. Transactions that are considered to threaten the competitive process can be prohibited altogether, or approved subject to 'remedies' such as an obligation to divest part of the merged business or to offer licences or access to facilities to enable other businesses to continue competing.

The substance and practice of _____ varies from jurisdiction to jurisdiction. Protecting the interests of consumers (consumer welfare) and ensuring that entrepreneurs have an opportunity to compete in the market economy are often treated as important objectives. _____ is closely connected with law on deregulation of access to markets, state aids and subsidies, the privatisation of state owned assets and the establishment of independent sector regulators. In recent decades, _____ has been viewed as a way to provide better public services.

a. Fee simple
c. Hostile work environment

b. Competition law
d. Due diligence

28.   In economics, a _____ exists when a specific individual or enterprise has sufficient control over a particular product or service to determine significantly the terms on which other individuals shall have access to it. Monopolies are thus characterized by a lack of economic competition for the good or service that they provide and a lack of viable substitute goods. The verb 'monopolize' refers to the process by which a firm gains persistently greater market share than what is expected under perfect competition.
   a. 130-30 fund
   c. 100-year flood

b. 1921 recession
d. Monopoly

29.   _____ is the transition of a national economy from monopoly control by groups of large businesses to a free market economy. This change rarely arises naturally, and is generally the result of regulation by a governing body.

A modern example of _____ is the economic restructuring of Germany after the fall of the Third Reich in 1945.

   a. Market power
   c. Monopolization

b. Complementary monopoly
d. Decartelization

30.   In microeconomics, _____ is quite simply the conversion of inputs into outputs. It is an economic process that uses resources to create a good or service that is suitable for exchange. This can include manufacturing, storing, shipping, and packaging.
   a. Red Guards
   c. MET

b. Production
d. Solved

1.   In game theory, _____ is a solution concept of a game involving two or more players, in which each player is assumed to know the equilibrium strategies of the other players, and no player has anything to gain by changing only his or her own strategy unilaterally. If each player has chosen a strategy and no player can benefit by changing his or her strategy while the other players keep theirs unchanged, then the current set of strategy choices and the corresponding payoffs constitute a _____.

Stated simply, Amy and Bill are in _____ if Amy is making the best decision she can, taking into account Bill's decision, and Bill is making the best decision he can, taking into account Amy's decision.

a. Nash equilibrium   b. Lump of labour
c. Proper equilibrium   d. Linear production game

2.   In game theory, a _____ is an extensive form game which consists in some number of repetitions of some base game (called a stage game.) The stage game is usually one of the well-studied 2-person games. It captures the idea that a player will have to take into account the impact of his current action on the future actions of other players; this is sometimes called his reputation.

a. Pursuit-evasion   b. Correlated equilibrium
c. Quasi-perfect equilibrium   d. Repeated game

3.   In game theory, a _____ is a game where one player chooses his action before the others choose theirs. Importantly, the later players must have some information of the first's choice, otherwise the difference in time would have no strategic effect. Extensive form representations are usually used for _____s, since they explicitly illustrate the sequential aspects of a game.

a. Conglomerate merger   b. Normative economics
c. Sequential game   d. Comparative economic systems

4.   _____ is an economic model used to describe an industry structure in which companies compete on the amount of output they will produce, which they decide on independently of each other and at the same time. It is named after Antoine Augustin Cournot (1801-1877) after he observed competition in a spring water duopoly. It has the following features:

- There is more than one firm and all firms produce a homogeneous product, i.e. there is no product differentiation;
- Firms do not cooperate, i.e. there is no collusion;
- Firms have market power, i.e. each firm's output decision affects the good's price;
- The number of firms is fixed;
- Firms compete in quantities, and choose quantities simultaneously;
- The firms are economically rational and act strategically, usually seeking to maximize profit given their competitors' decisions.

An essential assumption of this model is that each firm aims to maximize profits, based on the expectation that its own output decision will not have an effect on the decisions of its rivals. Price is a commonly known decreasing function of total output.

a. 130-30 fund   b. 1921 recession
c. 100-year flood   d. Cournot competition

5.   _____ refers to the objective and subjective components of the believability of a source or message.

Traditionally, _____ has two key components: trustworthiness and expertise, which both have objective and subjective components. Trustworthiness is a based more on subjective factors, but can include objective measurements such as established reliability.

a. 130-30 fund

b. Credibility

c. 100-year flood

d. 1921 recession

6.   This MAD scenario is often referred to as _____. The term deterrence was first used in this context after World War II; prior to that time, its use was limited to legal terminology.

In practice, the theory proved both utterly effective and exceptionally dangerous (e.g., Cuban Missile Crisis) through the end of the Cold War.

a. Berlin Wall

b. Mutual assured destruction

c. Sino-Soviet split

d. Nuclear Deterrence

7.   The _____ consists of a number of economic theories which describe the nature of the firm, company including its existence, its behaviour, and its relationship with the market.

In simplified terms, the _____ aims to answer these questions:

1.   Existence - why do firms emerge, why are not all transactions in the economy mediated over the market?
2.   Boundaries - why the boundary between firms and the market is located exactly there? Which transactions are performed internally and which are negotiated on the market?
3.   Organization - why are firms structured in such specific way? What is the interplay of formal and informal relationships?

Despite looking simple, these questions are not answered by the established economic theory, which usually views firms as given, and treats them as black boxes without any internal structure.

The First World War period saw a change of emphasis in economic theory away from industry-level analysis which mainly included analysing markets to analysis at the level of the firm, as it became increasingly clear that perfect competition was no longer an adequate model of how firms behaved. Economic theory till then had focussed on trying to understand markets alone and there had been little study on understanding why firms or organisations exist.

a. Khazzoom-Brookes postulate

b. Policy Ineffectiveness Proposition

c. Technology gap

d. Theory of the firm

8.   A _____ product is a product designed for cheapness and short-term convenience rather than medium to long-term durability, with most products only intended for single use. The term is also sometimes used for products that may last several months (ex. _____ air filters) to distinguish from similar products that last indefinitely (ex.

a. 1921 recession

b. 130-30 fund

c. 100-year flood

d. Disposable

9.   An _____ is a type of auction, whose most typical form is the 'open outcry' auction. The auctioneer opens the auction by announcing a Suggested Opening Bid, a starting price or reserve for the item on sale and then accepts increasingly higher bids from the floor consisting of buyers with a possible interest in the item. Unlike sealed bid auctions, 'open outcry' auctions are 'open' or fully transparent as the identity of all bidders is disclosed to each other bidder during the auction.

a. Auction sniping

b. Auction school

c. Online auction business model

d. English auction

10.

The _____ is an independent agency of the United States government, created, directed, and empowered by Congressional statute , and with the majority of its commissioners appointed by the current President. The _____ works towards six strategic goals in the areas of broadband, competition, the spectrum, the media, public safety and homeland security, and modernizing the _____.

a. 130-30 fund

b. Federal Communications Commission

c. 1921 recession

d. 100-year flood

11.   In finance, a _____ is a debt security, in which the authorized issuer owes the holders a debt and, depending on the terms of the _____, is obliged to pay interest (the coupon) and/or to repay the principal at a later date, termed maturity. A _____ is a formal contract to repay borrowed money with interest at fixed intervals.

Thus a _____ is like a loan: the issuer is the borrower (debtor), the holder is the lender (creditor), and the coupon is the interest.

a. Bond

b. Prize Bond

c. Zero-coupon

d. Callable

12.   A _____ is a type of auction where the auctioneer begins with a high asking price which is lowered until some participant is willing to accept the auctioneer's price, or a predetermined reserve price (the seller's minimum acceptable price) is reached. The winning participant pays the last announced price. This is also known as a 'clock auction' or an open-outcry descending-price auction.

a. Vickrey auction

b. French auction

c. Box social

d. Dutch auction

13.   In microeconomics, the reservation (or reserve) price is the maximum price a buyer is willing to pay for a good or service; or, conversely, the minimum price at which a seller is willing to sell a good or service. _____s are commonly used in auctions.

_____s vary for the buyer according to their disposable income, their desire for the good, and the prices of, and their information about substitute goods.

a. Mohring effect

b. Returns to scale

c. Producer surplus

d. Reservation price

14. _____ are conceptually similar to economies of scale. Whereas economies of scale primarily refer to efficiencies associated with supply-side changes, such as increasing or decreasing the scale of production, of a single product type, _____ refer to efficiencies primarily associated with demand-side changes, such as increasing or decreasing the scope of marketing and distribution, of different types of products. _____ are one of the main reasons for such marketing strategies as product bundling, product lining, and family branding.

a. Economies of scale

b. Economic production quantity

c. Isoquant

d. Economies of Scope

15. _____ in economics and business is the result of an exchange and from that trade we assign a numerical monetary value to a good, service or asset. If Alice trades Bob 4 apples for an orange, the _____ of an orange is 4 apples. Inversely, the _____ of an apple is 1/4 oranges.

a. Price war

b. Price

c. Price book

d. Premium pricing

16. _____ is an offer (often competitive) of setting a price one is willing to pay for something. A price offer is called a bid. The term may be used in context of auctions, stock exchange, card games, or real estate transactions.

a. Bord halfpenny

b. Normal good

c. Central limit order book

d. Bidding

17. _____ is an agreement, usually secretive, which occurs between two or more persons to deceive, mislead or to obtain an objective forbidden by law typically involving fraud or gaining an unfair advantage. It is an agreement among firms to divide the market, set prices kickbacks, or misrepresenting the independence of the relationship between the colluding parties.' All acts effected by _____ are considered void.

a. Net Book Agreement

b. Bid rigging

c. Collusion

d. Dividing territories

18. _____ are the inflation-indexed bonds issued by the U.S. Treasury. The principal is adjusted to the Consumer Price Index, the commonly used measure of inflation. The coupon rate is constant, but generates a different amount of interest when multiplied by the inflation-adjusted principal, thus protecting the holder against inflation.

a. 130-30 fund

b. Treasury Inflation-Protected Securities

c. 100-year flood

d. 1921 recession

19. _____ is a specific term used in companies' financial reporting from the company-whole point of view. Because that use excludes the effects of changing ownership interest, an economic measure of _____ is necessary for financial analysis from the shareholders' point of view

_____ is defined by the Financial Accounting Standards Board, or FASB, as e;the change in equity [net assets] of a business enterprise during a period from transactions and other events and circumstances from nonowner sources. It includes all changes in equity during a period except those resulting from investments by owners and distributions to owners.e;

_____ is the sum of net income and other items that must bypass the income statement because they have not been realized, including items like an unrealized holding gain or loss from available for sale securities and foreign currency translation gains or losses.

a. Net national income   b. Windfall gain

c. Comprehensive income   d. Real income

1. The _____ consists of a number of economic theories which describe the nature of the firm, company including its existence, its behaviour, and its relationship with the market.

In simplified terms, the _____ aims to answer these questions:

1. Existence - why do firms emerge, why are not all transactions in the economy mediated over the market?
2. Boundaries - why the boundary between firms and the market is located exactly there? Which transactions are performed internally and which are negotiated on the market?
3. Organization - why are firms structured in such specific way? What is the interplay of formal and informal relationships?

Despite looking simple, these questions are not answered by the established economic theory, which usually views firms as given, and treats them as black boxes without any internal structure.

The First World War period saw a change of emphasis in economic theory away from industry-level analysis which mainly included analysing markets to analysis at the level of the firm, as it became increasingly clear that perfect competition was no longer an adequate model of how firms behaved. Economic theory till then had focussed on trying to understand markets alone and there had been little study on understanding why firms or organisations exist.

a. Policy Ineffectiveness Proposition

b. Khazzoom-Brookes postulate

c. Technology gap

d. Theory of the firm

2. Economics:

- _____,the desire to own something and the ability to pay for it
- _____ curve,a graphic representation of a _____ schedule
- _____ deposit, the money in checking accounts
- _____ pull theory,the theory that inflation occurs when _____ for goods and services exceeds existing supplies
- _____ schedule,a table that lists the quantity of a good a person will buy it each different price
- _____ side economics,the school of economics at believes government spending and tax cuts open economy by raising _____

a. Demand

b. Variability

c. Production

d. McKesson ' Robbins scandal

3. _____ is a term in economics, where demand for one good or service occurs as a result of demand for another. This may occur as the former is a part of production of the second. For example, demand for coal leads to _____ for mining, as coal must be mined for coal to be consumed.

a. Derived demand

b. Rate risk

c. Leontief production function

d. Days Sales Outstanding

4. In microeconomics, _____ is the extra revenue that an additional unit of product will bring. It is the additional income from selling one more unit of a good; sometimes equal to price. It can also be described as the change in total revenue/change in number of units sold.

a. Long term   b. Reservation price
c. Market demand schedule   d. Marginal revenue

5.   The marginal revenue productivity theory of wages, also referred to as the _____ of labor, is the change in total revenue earned by a firm that results from employing one more unit of labor. It is a neoclassical model that determines, under some conditions, the optimal number of workers to employ at an exogenously determined market wage rate.

The _____ of a worker is equal to the product of the marginal product of labor (MP) and the marginal revenue (MR), given by MR×MP = _____.

a. Marginal revenue productivity theory of wages   b. Coal depletion
c. Real prices and ideal prices   d. Marginal revenue product

6.   _____ is the observation that people often do and believe things because many other people do and believe the same things. The effect is often pejoratively called herding instinct, particularly when applied to adolescents. People tend to follow the crowd without examining the merits of a particular thing.
a. Sunk costs   b. Hyperbolic discounting
c. Bandwagon effect   d. Halo effect

7.   In economics, the _____ can be defined as the graph depicting the relationship between the price of a certain commodity, and the amount of it that consumers are willing and able to purchase at that given price. It is a graphic representation of a demand schedule. The _____ for all consumers together follows from the _____ of every individual consumer: the individual demands at each price are added together.
a. Cost curve   b. Kuznets curve
c. Wage curve   d. Demand curve

8.   _____ is the term denoting either an entrance or changes which are inserted into a system and which activate/modify a process. It is an abstract concept, used in the modeling, system(s) design and system(s) exploitation. It is usually connected with other terms, e.g., _____ field, _____ variable, _____ parameter, _____ value, _____ signal, _____ device and _____ file.
a. ACEA agreement   b. AD-IA Model
c. ACCRA Cost of Living Index   d. Input

9.   In economics, _____ is the ratio of the percent change in one variable to the percent change in another variable. It is a tool for measuring the responsiveness of a function to changes in parameters in a relative way. Commonly analyzed are _____ of substitution, price and wealth.
a. Elasticity of demand   b. ACCRA Cost of Living Index
c. ACEA agreement   d. Elasticity

10.   Price _____ is defined as the measure of responsiveness in the quantity demanded for a commodity as a result of change in price of the same commodity. It is a measure of how consumers react to a change in price. In other words, it is percentage change in quantity demanded by the percentage change in price of the same commodity.
a. Elasticity   b. ACEA agreement
c. ACCRA Cost of Living Index   d. Elasticity of demand

11. _____ in economics and business is the result of an exchange and from that trade we assign a numerical monetary value to a good, service or asset. If Alice trades Bob 4 apples for an orange, the _____ of an orange is 4 apples. Inversely, the _____ of an apple is 1/4 oranges.

  a. Price book   b. Price war

  c. Premium pricing   d. Price

12. _____ is defined as the measure of responsiveness in the quantity demanded for a commodity as a result of change in price of the same commodity. It is a measure of how consumers react to a change in price. In other words, it is percentage change in quantity demanded as per the percentage change in price of the same commodity.

  a. 1921 recession   b. 130-30 fund

  c. 100-year flood   d. Price elasticity of demand

13. In economics, the concept of the _____ refers to the decision-making time frame of a firm in which at least one factor of production is fixed. Costs which are fixed in the _____ have no impact on a firms decisions. For example a firm can raise output by increasing the amount of labour through overtime.

  a. Productivity model   b. Short-run

  c. Hicks-neutral technical change   d. Product Pipeline

14. In economics, the _____ is defined as a numerical measure of the responsiveness of the quantity supplied of product (A) to a change in price of product (A) alone. It is the measure of the way quantity supplied reacts to a change in price.

For example, if, in response to a 10% rise in the price of a good, the quantity supplied increases by 20%, the _____ would be 20%/10% = 2.

  a. Demand shaping   b. Passive income

  c. Hedonimetry   d. Price elasticity of supply

15. In economics, the _____ is the wage rate that produces neither an access supply of workers nor an excess demand for workers and labor market. See economic equilibrium.

  a. Equilibrium wage   b. International free trade agreement

  c. Economic stability   d. Effective unemployment rate

16. Competitive market equilibrium is the traditional concept of economic equilibrium, appropriate for the analysis of commodity markets with flexible prices and many traders, and serving as the benchmark of efficiency in economic analysis. It relies crucially on the assumption of a competitive environment where each trader decides upon a quantity that is so small compared to the total quantity traded in the market that their individual transactions have no influence on the prices.Competitive markets are an ideal, a standard that other market structures are evaluated by.

A _____ consists of a vector of prices and an allocation such that given the prices, each trader by maximizing his objective function (profit, preferences) subject to his technological possibilities and resource constraints plans to trade into his part of the proposed allocation, and such that the prices make all net trades compatible with one another ('clear the market') by equating aggregate supply and demand for the commodities which are traded.

a. Market system
c. Product-Market Growth Matrix

b. Partial equilibrium
d. Competitive equilibrium

17.   The _____ is the number of total hours that workers wish to work at a given real wage rate.

Labor supply curves are derived from the 'labor-leisure' trade-off. More hours worked earn higher incomes but necessitate a cut in the amount of leisure that workers enjoy.

a. De minimis fringe benefits
c. Dual labor market

b. Compound interest
d. Supply of labor

18.   _____s is the social science that studies the production, distribution, and consumption of goods and services. The term _____s comes from the Ancient Greek oá¼°κονομῖα from oá¼¶κος (oikos, 'house') + νÏŒμος (nomos, 'custom' or 'law'), hence 'rules of the house(hold)'. Current _____ models developed out of the broader field of political economy in the late 19th century, owing to a desire to use an empirical approach more akin to the physical sciences.

a. Energy economics
c. Opportunity cost

b. Inflation
d. Economic

19.   In economics supernormal profit _____ or pure profit or excess profits, is a profit exceeding the normal profit. Normal profit equals the opportunity cost of labour and capital, while supernormal profit is the amount exceeds the normal return from these input factors in production.

_____ is usually generated by an oligopoly or a monopoly; however, these firms often try to hide this from the market to reduce risk of competition or antitrust investigation.

a. Economic profit
c. Abnormal profit

b. ACCRA Cost of Living Index
d. Accounting profit

20.   Economic _____ is defined as an excess distribution to any factor in a production process above that which is required to induce the factor into the process or any excess above that which is necessary to keep the factor in its current use..

Classical Factor _____ is primarily concerned with the fee paid for the use of fixed (e.g. natural) resources. The classical definition is expressed as any excess payment above that required to induce or provide for production.

a. 1921 recession
c. 100-year flood

b. 130-30 fund
d. Rent

21.   _____ or economic opportunity loss is the value of the next best alternative foregone as the result of making a decision. _____ analysis is an important part of a company's decision-making processes but is not treated as an actual cost in any financial statement. The next best thing that a person can engage in is referred to as the _____ of doing the best thing and ignoring the next best thing to be done.

a. Economic ideology
c. Economic

b. Opportunity cost
d. Industrial organization

22.   In economics, a _____ 'purchase') is a market form in which only one buyer faces many sellers. It is an example of imperfect competition, similar to a monopoly, in which only one seller faces many buyers. As the only purchaser of a good or service, the 'monopsonist' may dictate terms to its suppliers in the same manner that a monopolist controls the market for its buyers.

a. Monopsony
c. 1921 recession

b. 100-year flood
d. 130-30 fund

23.   _____ refers to a business or organization attempting to acquire goods or services to accomplish the goals of the enterprise. Though there are several organizations that attempt to set standards in the _____ process, processes can vary greatly between organizations. Typically the word '_____' is not used interchangeably with the word 'procurement', since procurement typically includes Expediting, Supplier Quality, and Traffic and Logistics (T'L) in addition to _____.

a. Free port
c. 130-30 fund

b. 100-year flood
d. Purchasing

24.   Competition law, known in the United States as _____ law, has three main elements:

- prohibiting agreements or practices that restrict free trading and competition between business entities. This includes in particular the repression of cartels.
- banning abusive behaviour by a firm dominating a market, or anti-competitive practices that tend to lead to such a dominant position. Practices controlled in this way may include predatory pricing, tying, price gouging, refusal to deal, and many others.
- supervising the mergers and acquisitions of large corporations, including some joint ventures. Transactions that are considered to threaten the competitive process can be prohibited altogether, or approved subject to 'remedies' such as an obligation to divest part of the merged business or to offer licences or access to facilities to enable other businesses to continue competing.

The substance and practice of competition law varies from jurisdiction to jurisdiction. Protecting the interests of consumers (consumer welfare) and ensuring that entrepreneurs have an opportunity to compete in the market economy are often treated as important objectives. Competition law is closely connected with law on deregulation of access to markets, state aids and subsidies, the privatisation of state owned assets and the establishment of independent sector regulators. In recent decades, competition law has been viewed as a way to provide better public services.

a. Intellectual property law
c. Anti-Inflation Act

b. Antitrust
d. United Kingdom competition law

25. _____, known in the United States as antitrust law, has three main elements:

- prohibiting agreements or practices that restrict free trading and competition between business entities. This includes in particular the repression of cartels.
- banning abusive behaviour by a firm dominating a market, or anti-competitive practices that tend to lead to such a dominant position. Practices controlled in this way may include predatory pricing, tying, price gouging, refusal to deal, and many others.
- supervising the mergers and acquisitions of large corporations, including some joint ventures. Transactions that are considered to threaten the competitive process can be prohibited altogether, or approved subject to 'remedies' such as an obligation to divest part of the merged business or to offer licences or access to facilities to enable other businesses to continue competing.

The substance and practice of _____ varies from jurisdiction to jurisdiction. Protecting the interests of consumers (consumer welfare) and ensuring that entrepreneurs have an opportunity to compete in the market economy are often treated as important objectives. _____ is closely connected with law on deregulation of access to markets, state aids and subsidies, the privatisation of state owned assets and the establishment of independent sector regulators. In recent decades, _____ has been viewed as a way to provide better public services.

a. Hostile work environment   b. Due diligence
c. Fee simple   d. Competition law

26. A _____ is a counterfeit agreement among industries. It is an informal organization of producers that agree to coordinate prices and production. _____s usually occur in an oligopolistic industry, where there is a small number of sellers and usually involve homogeneous products.
a. Shill   b. 100-year flood
c. Shanzhai   d. Cartel

27. _____ describes a deliberate attempt to interfere with the free and fair operation of the market and create artificial, false or misleading appearances with respect to the price of a security, commodity or currency. _____ is prohibited under Section 9(a)(2) of the Securities Exchange Act of 1934, and in Australia under Section s 1041A of the Corporations Act 2001. The Act defines _____ as transactions which create an artificial price or maintain an artificial price for a tradable security.
a. Legal monopoly   b. Market manipulation
c. Managerial economics   d. Net domestic product

28. A _____ is the lowest hourly, daily or monthly wage that employers may legally pay to employees or workers. Equivalently, it is the lowest wage at which workers may sell their labor. Although _____ laws are in effect in a great many jurisdictions, there are differences of opinion about the benefits and drawbacks of a _____.
a. Permanent war economy   b. Microfoundations
c. Marginal propensity to consume   d. Minimum wage

29.   In economics, a _____ exists when a specific individual or enterprise has sufficient control over a particular product or service to determine significantly the terms on which other individuals shall have access to it. Monopolies are thus characterized by a lack of economic competition for the good or service that they provide and a lack of viable substitute goods. The verb 'monopolize' refers to the process by which a firm gains persistently greater market share than what is expected under perfect competition.

   a. Monopoly   b. 100-year flood

   c. 130-30 fund   d. 1921 recession

30.   In economics, the _____ is that part of the economy which is both run for private profit and is not controlled by the state. By contrast, enterprises that are part of the state are part of the public sector; private, non-profit organizations are regarded as part of the voluntary sector.

A variety of legal structures exist for _____ business organizations, depending on the jurisdiction in which they have their legal domicile.

   a. Secondary sector of the economy   b. Primary products

   c. Standard Industrial Classification   d. Private sector

1. _____ measures the nominal future sum of money that a given sum of money is 'worth' at a specified time in the future assuming a certain interest rate rate of return; it is the present value multiplied by the accumulation function.

The value does not include corrections for inflation or other factors that affect the true value of money in the future. This is used in time value of money calculations.

a. Future-oriented	b. Future value
c. Negative gearing	d. Present value

2. _____ is a fee paid on borrowed assets. It is the price paid for the use of borrowed money , or, money earned by deposited funds . Assets that are sometimes lent with _____ include money, shares, consumer goods through hire purchase, major assets such as aircraft, and even entire factories in finance lease arrangements.

a. Interest	b. Internal debt
c. Asset protection	d. Insolvency

3. An _____ is the price a borrower pays for the use of money they do not own, for instance a small company might borrow from a bank to kick start their business, and the return a lender receives for deferring the use of funds, by lending it to the borrower. _____s are normally expressed as a percentage rate over the period of one year.

_____s targets are also a vital tool of monetary policy and are used to control variables like investment, inflation, and unemployment.

a. Enterprise value	b. Arrow-Debreu model
c. ACCRA Cost of Living Index	d. Interest rate

4. _____ is the a method of technical and economic research of the systems for purpose to optimize a parity between system's consumer functions or properties and expenses to achieve those functions or properties.

This methodology for continuous perfection of production, industrial technologies, organizational structures was developed by Juryj Sobolev in 1948 at the 'Perm telephone factory'

- 1948 Juryj Sobolev - the first success in application of a method analysis at the 'Perm telephone factory' .
- 1949 - the first application for the invention as result of use of the new method.

Today in economically developed countries practically each enterprise or the company use methodology of the kind of functional-cost analysis as a practice of the quality management, most full satisfying to principles of standards of series ISO 9000.

- Interest of consumer not in products itself, but the advantage which it will receive from its usage.
- The consumer aspires to reduce his expenses
- Functions needed by consumer can be executed in the various ways, and, hence, with various efficiency and expenses. Among possible alternatives of realization of functions exist such in which the parity of quality and the price is the optimal for the consumer.

The goal of _____ is achievement of the highest consumer satisfaction of production at simultaneous decrease in all kinds of industrial expenses Classical _____ has three English synonyms - Value Engineering, Value Management, Value Analysis.

a. Staple financing

c. Monopoly wage

b. Willingness to pay

d. Function cost analysis

5. _____ is a term used in economics and game theory to describe an economic situation or game in which knowledge about other market participants or players is available to all participants. Every player knows the payoffs and strategies available to other players.

_____ is one of the theoretical pre-conditions of an efficient perfectly competitive market.

a. Complete information

c. Replicator equation

b. Repeated game

d. Metagame analysis

6. _____ is a specific term used in companies' financial reporting from the company-whole point of view. Because that use excludes the effects of changing ownership interest, an economic measure of _____ is necessary for financial analysis from the shareholders' point of view

_____ is defined by the Financial Accounting Standards Board, or FASB, as e;the change in equity [net assets] of a business enterprise during a period from transactions and other events and circumstances from nonowner sources. It includes all changes in equity during a period except those resulting from investments by owners and distributions to owners.e;

_____ is the sum of net income and other items that must bypass the income statement because they have not been realized, including items like an unrealized holding gain or loss from available for sale securities and foreign currency translation gains or losses.

a. Comprehensive income

c. Windfall gain

b. Net national income

d. Real income

7. In finance, a _____ is a debt security, in which the authorized issuer owes the holders a debt and, depending on the terms of the _____, is obliged to pay interest (the coupon) and/or to repay the principal at a later date, termed maturity. A _____ is a formal contract to repay borrowed money with interest at fixed intervals.

Thus a _____ is like a loan: the issuer is the borrower (debtor), the holder is the lender (creditor), and the coupon is the interest.

a. Bond

c. Zero-coupon

b. Prize Bond

d. Callable

8. A _____ is an annuity that has no definite end, or a stream of cash payments that continues forever. There are few actual perpetuities in existence (although the British government has issued them in the past, and they are known and still trade as consols.) A number of types of investments are effectively perpetuities, such as real estate and preferred stock, and techniques for valuing a _____ can be applied to establish price.

     a. Heath-Jarrow-Morton framework   b. Perpetuity

     c. Discount rate   d. Current yield

9. _____ is the value on a given date of a future payment or series of future payments, discounted to reflect the time value of money and other factors such as investment risk. _____ calculations are widely used in business and economics to provide a means to compare cash flows at different times on a meaningful 'like to like' basis.

Money value fluctuates over time: $100 today are not worth $100 in five years.

     a. Future value   b. Present value of costs

     c. Tax shield   d. Present value

10. _____ refers to the movement of cash into or out of a business or financial product. It is usually measured during a specified, finite period of time. Measurement of _____ can be used

- to determine a project's rate of return or value. The time of _____s into and out of projects are used as inputs in financial models such as internal rate of return, and net present value.
- to determine problems with a business's liquidity. Being profitable does not necessarily mean being liquid. A company can fail because of a shortage of cash, even while profitable.
- as an alternate measure of a business's profits when it is believed that accrual accounting concepts do not represent economic realities. For example, a company may be notionally profitable but generating little operational cash (as may be the case for a company that barters its products rather than selling for cash.) In such a case, the company may be deriving additional operating cash by issuing shares evaluating default risk, re-investment requirements, etc.

_____ is a generic term used differently depending on the context. It may be defined by users for their own purposes.

     a. Strip financing   b. Restricted stock

     c. Second lien loan   d. Cash flow

11. In finance, _____ rate of profit or sometimes just return, is the ratio of money gained or lost on an investment relative to the amount of money invested. The amount of money gained or lost may be referred to as interest, profit/loss, gain/loss, or net income/loss. The money invested may be referred to as the asset, capital, principal, or the cost basis of the investment.

     a. Current ratio   b. Cost accrual ratio

     c. Sortino ratio   d. Rate of return

12. A _____ is a bond issued by a corporation. It is a bond that a corporation issues to raise money in order to expand its business. The term is usually applied to longer-term debt instruments, generally with a maturity date falling at least a year after their issue date.

a. Dirty price

b. Bond fund

c. Bond valuation

d. Corporate bond

13.   Discounting is a financial mechanism in which a debtor obtains the right to delay payments to a creditor, for a defined period of time, in exchange for a charge or fee. Essentially, the party that owes money in the present purchases the right to delay the payment until some future date. The _____, or charge, is simply the difference between the original amount owed in the present and the amount that has to be paid in the future to settle the debt.

a. Reinsurance

b. Discount

c. Certified Risk Manager

d. Reliability theory

14.   The _____ is an interest rate a central bank charges depository institutions that borrow reserves from it.

The term _____ has two meanings:

- the same as interest rate; the term 'discount' does not refer to the meaning of the word, but to the purpose of using the quantity, such as computations of present value, e.g. net present value or discounted cash flow

- the annual effective _____, which is the annual interest divided by the capital including that interest; this rate is lower than the interest rate; it corresponds to using the value after a year as the nominal value, and seeing the initial value as the nominal value minus a discount; it is used for Treasury Bills and similar financial instruments

The annual effective _____ is the annual interest divided by the capital including that interest, which is the interest rate divided by 100% plus the interest rate. It is the annual discount factor to be applied to the future cash flow, to find the discount, subtracted from a future value to find the value one year earlier.

For example, suppose there is a government bond that sells for $95 and pays $100 in a year's time.

a. Perpetuity

b. Johansen test

c. Discount rate

d. Stochastic volatility

15.   _____ or net present worth (NPW) is defined as the total present value (PV) of a time series of cash flows. It is a standard method for using the time value of money to appraise long-term projects. Used for capital budgeting, and widely throughout economics, it measures the excess or shortfall of cash flows, in present value terms, once financing charges are met.

a. Net present value

b. Future value

c. Refinancing risk

d. Maturity

16.   _____ are made by investors and investment managers.

Investors commonly perform investment analysis by making use of fundamental analysis, technical analysis and gut feel.

_____ are often supported by decision tools.

a. Investment decisions   b. Arbitrage betting
c. Investment strategy   d. Inventory investment

17. _____ or economic opportunity loss is the value of the next best alternative foregone as the result of making a decision. _____ analysis is an important part of a company's decision-making processes but is not treated as an actual cost in any financial statement. The next best thing that a person can engage in is referred to as the _____ of doing the best thing and ignoring the next best thing to be done.
   a. Economic   b. Economic ideology
   c. Industrial organization   d. Opportunity cost

18. The _____ is an expected return that the provider of capital plans to earn on their investment.

Capital (money) used for funding a business should earn returns for the capital providers who risk their capital. For an investment to be worthwhile, the expected return on capital must be greater than the _____.

   a. Modigliani-Miller theorem   b. Cost of Capital
   c. Capital intensive   d. Capital expenditure

19. The _____ is the expected return forgone by bypassing of other potential investment activities for a given capital. It is a rate of return that investors could earn in financial markets.
   a. ACCRA Cost of Living Index   b. AD-IA Model
   c. ACEA agreement   d. Opportunity cost of Capital

20. A _____ is the minimum difference a person requires to be willing to take an uncertain bet, between the expected value of the bet and the certain value that he is indifferent to.

The certainty equivalent is the guaranteed payoff at which a person is 'indifferent' between accepting the guaranteed payoff and a higher but uncertain payoff. (It is the amount of the higher payout minus the _____.)

   a. Ruin theory   b. Workers compensation
   c. Risk premium   d. Linear model

21. In business and accounting, _____ are everything of value that is owned by a person or company. It is a claim on the property your income of a borrower. The balance sheet of a firm records the monetary value of the _____ owned by the firm.
   a. ACEA agreement   b. ACCRA Cost of Living Index
   c. Amortization schedule   d. Assets

22.   The term _____ has three unrelated technical definitions, and is also used in a variety of non-technical ways.

- In financial economics, it refers to any asset used to make money, as opposed to assets used for personal enjoyment or consumption. This is an important distinction because two people can disagree sharply about the value of personal assets, one person might think a sports car is more valuable than a pickup truck, another person might have the opposite taste. But if an asset is held for the purpose of making money, taste has nothing to do with it, only differences of opinion about how much money the asset will produce. With the further assumption that people agree on the probability distribution of future cash flows, it is possible to have an objective _____ pricing model. Even without the assumption of agreement, it is possible to set rational limits on _____ value.
- In governmental accounting, it is defined as any asset used in operations with an initial useful life extending beyond one reporting period. Generally, government managers have a 'stewardship' duty to maintain _____s under their control. See International Public Sector Accounting Standards for details.
- In US tax accounting, it is defined as any property other than a list of exceptions. The main exceptions are anything held for sale, and any real estate or depreciable property used in business. Almost everything you own and use for personal purposes, pleasure or investment is a _____. If something is a _____ for tax purposes, gains or losses on sale or disposition are capital gains or capital losses. For individuals, however, capital losses on property held for personal use are generally not deductible. See the IRS publication Tax Facts about Capital Gains and Losses for details.

A well-known financial accounting textbook advises that the term be avoided except in tax accounting because it is used in so many different senses, not all of them well-defined. For example it is often used as a synonym for fixed assets or for investments in securities.

A common non-technical usage occurs when people ask that employees or the environment or something else be treated as a _____.

a. Capital Asset

b. Dynamic asset allocation

c. Consumption beta

d. Mid price

23.   In finance, the _____ is used to determine a theoretically appropriate required rate of return of an asset, if that asset is to be added to an already well-diversified portfolio, given that asset's non-diversifiable risk. The model takes into account the asset's sensitivity to non-diversifiable risk (also known as systemic risk or market risk), often represented by the quantity beta (β) in the financial industry, as well as the expected return of the market and the expected return of a theoretical risk-free asset.

The model was introduced by Jack Treynor (1961, 1962), William Sharpe (1964), John Lintner (1965a,b) and Jan Mossin (1966) independently, building on the earlier work of Harry Markowitz on diversification and modern portfolio theory.

a. Ho-Lee model

b. Martingale pricing

c. Fama-MacBeth regression

d. Capital Asset Pricing Model

24.   _____ refers to the stock of skills and knowledge embodied in the ability to perform labor so as to produce economic value. It is the skills and knowledge gained by a worker through education and experience.Many early economic theories refer to it simply as labor, one of three factors of production, and consider it to be a fungible resource -- homogeneous and easily interchangeable. Other conceptions of labor dispense with these assumptions.

a. General equilibrium
c. Price theory

b. Law of increasing costs
d. Human capital

25. _____ is one of the four Ps of the marketing mix. The other three aspects are product, promotion, and place. It is also a key variable in microeconomic price allocation theory.

a. Point of total assumption
c. Pricing

b. Guaranteed Maximum Price
d. Premium pricing

26. The _____ consists of a number of economic theories which describe the nature of the firm, company including its existence, its behaviour, and its relationship with the market.

In simplified terms, the _____ aims to answer these questions:

1. Existence - why do firms emerge, why are not all transactions in the economy mediated over the market?
2. Boundaries - why the boundary between firms and the market is located exactly there? Which transactions are performed internally and which are negotiated on the market?
3. Organization - why are firms structured in such specific way? What is the interplay of formal and informal relationships?

Despite looking simple, these questions are not answered by the established economic theory, which usually views firms as given, and treats them as black boxes without any internal structure.

The First World War period saw a change of emphasis in economic theory away from industry-level analysis which mainly included analysing markets to analysis at the level of the firm, as it became increasingly clear that perfect competition was no longer an adequate model of how firms behaved. Economic theory till then had focussed on trying to understand markets alone and there had been little study on understanding why firms or organisations exist.

a. Khazzoom-Brookes postulate
c. Technology gap

b. Theory of the firm
d. Policy Ineffectiveness Proposition

27. A _____ product is a product designed for cheapness and short-term convenience rather than medium to long-term durability, with most products only intended for single use. The term is also sometimes used for products that may last several months (ex. _____ air filters) to distinguish from similar products that last indefinitely (ex.

a. 1921 recession
c. 100-year flood

b. Disposable
d. 130-30 fund

28. Procter is a surname, and may also refer to:

- Bryan Waller Procter (pseud. Barry Cornwall), English poet
- Goodwin Procter, American law firm
- _____, consumer products multinational

a. Bucket shop

c. Tightness

b. Drawdown

d. Procter ' Gamble

29. _____ is a broad label that refers to any individuals or households that use goods and services generated within the economy. The concept of a _____ is used in different contexts, so that the usage and significance of the term may vary.

Typically when business people and economists talk of _____s they are talking about person as _____, an aggregated commodity item with little individuality other than that expressed in the buy/not-buy decision.

a. 130-30 fund

c. 1921 recession

b. 100-year flood

d. Consumer

30. _____ is the study of when, why, how, where and what people do or do not buy products. It blends elements from psychology, sociology,social psychology, anthropology and economics. It attempts to understand the buyer decision making process, both individually and in groups.

a. Consumer behavior

c. Shopping Neutral

b. Situational theory of publics

d. Consumption smoothing

31. _____ is the term denoting either an entrance or changes which are inserted into a system and which activate/modify a process. It is an abstract concept, used in the modeling, system(s) design and system(s) exploitation. It is usually connected with other terms, e.g., _____ field, _____ variable, _____ parameter, _____ value, _____ signal, _____ device and _____ file.

a. ACEA agreement

c. ACCRA Cost of Living Index

b. AD-IA Model

d. Input

32. _____ in economics and business is the result of an exchange and from that trade we assign a numerical monetary value to a good, service or asset. If Alice trades Bob 4 apples for an orange, the _____ of an orange is 4 apples. Inversely, the _____ of an apple is 1/4 oranges.

a. Premium pricing

c. Price war

b. Price book

d. Price

33. In economics, a _____ may be either a subsidy or a price control, both with the intended effect of keeping the market price of a good higher than the competitive equilibrium level.

In the case of a price control, a _____ is the minimum legal price a seller may charge, typically placed above equilibrium. It is the support of certain price levels at or above market values by the government.

a. Payment schedule

c. Labor intensity

b. Marginal profit

d. Price support

34. In microeconomics, _____ is quite simply the conversion of inputs into outputs. It is an economic process that uses resources to create a good or service that is suitable for exchange. This can include manufacturing, storing, shipping, and packaging.

a. Red Guards   b. MET

c. Solved   d. Production

35. _____ is an economic concept with commonplace familiarity. It is the price that a good or service is offered at, or will fetch, in the marketplace. It is of interest mainly in the study of microeconomics.

a. Paper trading   b. Market anomaly

c. Market price   d. Noisy market hypothesis

36. The Organization of the Petroleum Exporting Countries is a cartel of twelve countries made up of Algeria, Angola, Ecuador, Iran, Iraq, Kuwait, Libya, Nigeria, Qatar, Saudi Arabia, the United Arab Emirates, and Venezuela. The cartel has maintained its headquarters in Vienna since 1965, and hosts regular meetings among the oil ministers of its Member Countries. Indonesia withdrew its membership in _____ in 2008 after it became a net importer of oil, but stated it would likely return if it became a net exporter in the world.

a. AD-IA Model   b. ACEA agreement

c. ACCRA Cost of Living Index   d. OPEC

37.   A _____ is:

- Rewrite _____, in generative grammar and computer science
- Standardization, a formal and widely-accepted statement, fact, definition, or qualification
- Operation, a determinate _____ for performing a mathematical operation and obtaining a certain result (Mathematics, Logic)
    - Unary operation
    - Binary operation
- _____ of inference, a function from sets of formulae to formulae (Mathematics, Logic)
- _____ of thumb, principle with broad application that is not intended to be strictly accurate or reliable for every situation. Also often simply referred to as a _____
- Moral, an atomic element of a moral code for guiding choices in human behavior
- Heuristic, a quantized '_____' which shows a tendency or probability for successful function
- A regulation, as in sports
- A Production _____, as in computer science
- Procedural law, a _____ set governing the application of laws to cases
    - A law, which may informally be called a '_____'
    - A court ruling, a decision by a court
- In the U.S. Government, a regulation mandated by Congress, but written or expanded upon by the Executive Branch.
- Norm (sociology), an informal but widely accepted _____, concept, truth, definition, or qualification (social norms, legal norms, coding norms)
- Norm (philosophy), a kind of sentence or a reason to act, feel or believe
- 'Rulership' is the concept of governance by a government:
    - Military _____, governance by a military body
    - Monastic _____, a collection of precepts that guides the life of monks or nuns in a religious order where the superior holds the place of Christ
- Slide _____

- '_____,' a song by Ayumi Hamasaki
- '_____,' a song by rapper Nas
- '_____s,' an album by the band The Whitest Boy Alive
- _____s: Pyaar Ka Superhit Formula, a 2003 Bollywood film
- ruler, an instrument for measuring lengths
- _____, a component of an astrolabe, circumferator or similar instrument
- The _____s, a bestselling self-help book
- _____ Project (Run Up-to-date Linux Everywhere), a project that aims to use up-to-date Linux software on old PCs
- _____ engine, a software system that helps managing business _____s
- Ja _____, a hip hop artist
    - R.U.L.E., a 2005 greatest hits album by rapper Ja _____
- '_____s,' a KMFDM song

a. Procter ' Gamble   b. Rule

c. Demand   d. Technocracy

38. In economics, _____ is the process by which a firm determines the price and output level that returns the greatest profit. There are several approaches to this problem. The total revenue--total cost method relies on the fact that profit equals revenue minus cost, and the marginal revenue--marginal cost method is based on the fact that total profit in a perfectly competitive market reaches its maximum point where marginal revenue equals marginal cost.

a. Profit margin

b. Normal profit

c. 100-year flood

d. Profit maximization

39. In economics, the _____ market is a hypothetical market that brings savers and borrowers together, also bringing together the money available in commercial banks and lending institutions available for firms and households to finance expenditures, either investments or consumption. Savers supply the _____; for instance, buying bonds will transfer their money to the institution issuing the bond, which can be a firm or government. In return, borrowers demand _____; when an institution sells a bond, it is demanding _____.

a. Loanable funds

b. Reservation wage

c. Spatial inequality

d. Buffer stock scheme

40. Economics:

- _____,the desire to own something and the ability to pay for it
- _____ curve,a graphic representation of a _____ schedule
- _____ deposit, the money in checking accounts
- _____ pull theory,the theory that inflation occurs when _____ for goods and services exceeds existing supplies
- _____ schedule,a table that lists the quantity of a good a person will buy it each different price
- _____ side economics,the school of economics at believes government spending and tax cuts open economy by raising _____

a. Production

b. Demand

c. McKesson ' Robbins scandal

d. Variability

41. In the United States, _____ are overnight borrowings by banks to maintain their bank reserves at the Federal Reserve. Banks keep reserves at Federal Reserve Banks to meet their reserve requirements and to clear financial transactions. Transactions in the _____ market enable depository institutions with reserve balances in excess of reserve requirements to lend reserves to institutions with reserve deficiencies.

a. Federal funds rate

b. Federal funds

c. Federal Reserve Transparency Act

d. Term auction facility

42. In the United States, the _____ is the interest rate at which private depository institutions (mostly banks) lend balances (federal funds) at the Federal Reserve to other depository institutions, usually overnight. It is the interest rate banks charge each other for loans. Changing the target rate is one way the Chairman of the Federal Reserve can influence the supply of money in the U.S. economy..

a. Monetary Policy Report to the Congress

b. Federal funds rate

c. Federal banking

d. Term auction facility

43. _____ is a term applied in many countries to a reference interest rate used by banks. The term originally indicated the rate of interest at which banks lent to favored customers, i.e., those with high credibility, though this is no longer always the case. Some variable interest rates may be expressed as a percentage above or below _____.

   a. Repo Rate   b. Capital requirement

   c. Prime rate   d. Transactional account

44. A _____ is a rate that determines pay-offs in a financial contract and that is outside the control of the parties to the contract. It is often some form of LIBOR rate, but it can take many forms, such as a consumer price index, a house price index or an unemployment rate. Parties to the contract choose a _____ that neither party has power to manipulate.

   a. Shanghai Interbank Offered Rate   b. London Interbank Offered Rate

   c. Reference rate   d. SIBOR

1. _____ theory is a branch of theoretical economics. It seeks to explain the behavior of supply, demand and prices in a whole economy with several or many markets. It is often assumed that agents are price takers and in that setting two common notions of equilibrium exist: Walrasian (or competitive) equilibrium, and its generalization; a price equilibrium with transfers.

   a. New Keynesian economics   b. Rational choice theory
   c. Human capital   d. General equilibrium

2. A _____ is a type of economic equilibrium, where the clearance on the market of some specific goods is obtained independently from prices and quantities demanded and supplied in other markets. In other words, the prices of all substitutes and complements, as well as income levels of consumers are constant. Here the dynamic process is that prices adjust until supply equals demand.

   a. Market depth   b. Partial equilibrium
   c. Market system   d. Horizontal market

3. In economics, the _____ is the rate at which a consumer is ready to give up one good in exchange for another good while maintaining the same level of satisfaction.

   Under the standard assumption of neoclassical economics that goods and services are continuously divisible, the marginal rates of substitution will be the same regardless of the direction of exchange, and will correspond to the slope of an indifference curve (more precisely, to the slope multiplied by -1) passing through the consumption bundle in question, at that point: mathematically, it is the implicit derivative. MRS of Y for X is the amount of Y for which a consumer is willing to exchange for X locally.

   a. Supply and demand   b. Demand vacuum
   c. Quality bias   d. Marginal rate of substitution

4. _____ is an important concept in economics with broad applications in game theory, engineering and the social sciences. The term is named after Vilfredo Pareto, an Italian economist who used the concept in his studies of economic efficiency and income distribution. Informally, pareto efficient situations are those in which any change to make any person better off would make someone else worse off.

   a. Perfect rationality   b. Matching pennies
   c. Lump of labour   d. Pareto efficiency

5. In economics, an _____ is a way of representing various distributions of resources. Edgeworth made his presentation in his famous book, Mathematical Psychics: An essay on the application of mathematics to the moral sciences, 1881. Edgeworth's original two axis depiction was developed into the now familiar box diagram by Pareto in 1906 and was popularized in a later exposition by Bowley.

   a. Edgeworth box   b. International Social Security Association
   c. Equivalent variation   d. ACCRA Cost of Living Index

6. Given some endowment in an Edgeworth box, the _____ is the individually rational subset of the Pareto set. In other words, it is the set of Pareto efficient allocations in an economy. Also, any Walrasian equilibrium lies in the _____ of the Pareto set.

   a. Contract curve   b. Missing market
   c. Hidden Welfare State   d. Social welfare function

7. _____ is a broad label that refers to any individuals or households that use goods and services generated within the economy. The concept of a _____ is used in different contexts, so that the usage and significance of the term may vary.

Typically when business people and economists talk of _____s they are talking about person as _____, an aggregated commodity item with little individuality other than that expressed in the buy/not-buy decision.

a. 100-year flood
c. 130-30 fund

b. 1921 recession
d. Consumer

8. _____ is the study of when, why, how, where and what people do or do not buy products. It blends elements from psychology, sociology,social psychology, anthropology and economics. It attempts to understand the buyer decision making process, both individually and in groups.

a. Consumption smoothing
c. Situational theory of publics

b. Consumer behavior
d. Shopping Neutral

9. In economics, economic equilibrium is simply a state of the world where economic forces are balanced and in the absence of external influences the (equilibrium) values of economic variables will not change. It is the point at which quantity demanded and quantity supplied are equal. _____, for example, refers to a condition where a market price is established through competition such that the amount of goods or services sought by buyers is equal to the amount of goods or services produced by sellers.

a. Product-Market Growth Matrix
c. Marketization

b. Regulated market
d. Market Equilibrium

10. Economics:

- _____,the desire to own something and the ability to pay for it
- _____ curve,a graphic representation of a _____ schedule
- _____ deposit, the money in checking accounts
- _____ pull theory,the theory that inflation occurs when _____ for goods and services exceeds existing supplies
- _____ schedule,a table that lists the quantity of a good a person will buy it each different price
- _____ side economics,the school of economics at believes government spending and tax cuts open economy by raising _____

a. Variability
c. McKesson ' Robbins scandal

b. Production
d. Demand

11. In economics, _____ is when quantity demanded is more than quantity supplied.See Economic shortage.
a. ACCRA Cost of Living Index
c. Excess demand

b. AD-IA Model
d. ACEA agreement

12. In economics, _____ is when quantity supplied is more than quantity demanded. .

a. Effective unemployment rate

b. Illicit financial flows

c. Economic Value Creation

d. Excess supply

13. _____ is the observation that people often do and believe things because many other people do and believe the same things. The effect is often pejoratively called herding instinct, particularly when applied to adolescents. People tend to follow the crowd without examining the merits of a particular thing.

a. Hyperbolic discounting

b. Bandwagon effect

c. Sunk costs

d. Halo effect

14. _____ was a survey conducted by the U.S. Department of Justice to gauge the prevalence of alcohol and illegal drug use among prior arrestees. It was a reformulation of the prior Drug Use Forecasting (DUF) program, focused on five drugs in particular: cocaine, marijuana, methamphetamine, opiates, and PCP.

Participants were randomly selected from arrest records in major metropolitan areas; because no personally identifying information is taken from each record chosen, the resulting data can be correlated to arrest rates, but not to the total population of persons charged.

a. AD-IA Model

b. ACCRA Cost of Living Index

c. ACEA agreement

d. Arrestee Drug Abuse Monitoring

15. _____s is the social science that studies the production, distribution, and consumption of goods and services. The term _____s comes from the Ancient Greek oá¼°κονομῖα from oá¼¶κος (oikos, 'house') + vÏŒμος (nomos, 'custom' or 'law'), hence 'rules of the house(hold)'. Current _____ models developed out of the broader field of political economy in the late 19th century, owing to a desire to use an empirical approach more akin to the physical sciences.

a. Inflation

b. Energy economics

c. Opportunity cost

d. Economic

16. _____ is used to refer to a number of related concepts. It is the using resources in such a way as to maximize the production of goods and services. A system can be called economically efficient if:

- No one can be made better off without making someone else worse off.
- More output cannot be obtained without increasing the amount of inputs.
- Production proceeds at the lowest possible per-unit cost.

These definitions of efficiency are not equivalent, but they are all encompassed by the idea that nothing more can be achieved given the resources available.

An economic system is more efficient if it can provide more goods and services for society without using more resources.

a. Economic efficiency

b. ACCRA Cost of Living Index

c. ACEA agreement

d. Efficient contract theory

17. In economics, the _____ is the term economists use to describe the self-regulating nature of the marketplace. The _____ is a metaphor coined by the economist Adam Smith in The Wealth of Nations.

Adam Smith mentions the metaphor in Book IV of The Wealth of Nations, arguing that people in any society will certainly employ their capital in foreign trading only if the profits available by that method far exceed those available locally, and that in such a case it is better for society as a whole if they so did.

a. ACEA agreement

b. Invisible hand

c. ACCRA Cost of Living Index

d. AD-IA Model

18. _____ was a Scottish moral philosopher and a pioneer of political economy. One of the key figures of the Scottish Enlightenment, Smith is the author of The Theory of Moral Sentiments and An Inquiry into the Nature and Causes of the Wealth of Nations. The latter, usually abbreviated as The Wealth of Nations, is considered his magnum opus and the first modern work of economics.

a. Adolf Hitler

b. Adam Smith

c. Adolph Fischer

d. Alan Greenspan

19. _____ is a branch of economics that uses microeconomic techniques to simultaneously determine allocative efficiency within an economy and the income distribution associated with it. It analyzes social welfare, however measured, in terms of economic activities of the individuals that comprise the theoretical society considered. As such, individuals, with associated economic activities, are the basic units for aggregating to social welfare, whether of a group, a community, or a society, and there is no 'social welfare' apart from the 'welfare' associated with its individual units.

a. Law of increasing costs

b. General equilibrium

c. Tobit model

d. Welfare economics

20. In economics, and cost accounting, _____ describes the total economic cost of production and is made up of variable costs, which vary according to the quantity of a good produced and include inputs such as labor and raw materials, plus fixed costs, which are independent of the quantity of a good produced and include inputs (capital) that cannot be varied in the short term, such as buildings and machinery. _____ in economics includes the total opportunity cost of each factor of production in addition to fixed and variable costs.

The rate at which _____ changes as the amount produced changes is called marginal cost.

a. 130-30 fund

b. 100-year flood

c. 1921 recession

d. Total cost

21. _____ is the concept or idea of fairness in economics, particularly as to taxation or welfare economics.

In welfare economics, _____ may be distinguished from economic efficiency in overall evaluation of social welfare. Although '_____' has broader uses, it may be posed as a counterpart to economic inequality in yielding a 'good' distribution of welfare.

a. ACEA agreement

b. Equity

c. AD-IA Model

d. ACCRA Cost of Living Index

22. In economics, _____ is a measure of the relative satisfaction from consumption of various goods and services. Given this measure, one may speak meaningfully of increasing or decreasing _____, and thereby explain economic behavior in terms of attempts to increase one's _____. For illustrative purposes, changes in _____ are sometimes expressed in units called utils.

   a. Utility
   b. Utility function
   c. Ordinal utility
   d. Expected utility hypothesis

23. A _____ provision refers to any program which seeks to provide a minimum level of income, service or other support for many marginalized groups such as the poor, elderly, and disabled people. _____ programs are undertaken by governments as well as non-governmental organizations (NGOs.) _____ payments and services are typically provided at the expense of taxpayers generally, funded by benefactors, or by compulsory enrollment of the poor themselves.

   a. 130-30 fund
   b. Social welfare
   c. 100-year flood
   d. 1921 recession

24. In economics, a _____ is a real-valued function that ranks conceivable social states (alternative complete descriptions of the society) from lowest to highest. Inputs of the function include any variables considered to affect welfare of the society (Sen, 1970, p. 33.)

   a. Contract curve
   b. Social welfare function
   c. Frisch elasticity of labor supply
   d. Gini coefficient

25. In neoclassical economics and microeconomics, _____ describes the perfect being a market in which there are many small firms, all producing homogeneous goods. In the short term, such markets are productively inefficient as output will not occur where mc is equal to ac, but allocatively efficient, as output under _____ will always occur where mc is equal to mr, and therefore where mc equals ar. However, in the long term, such markets are both allocatively and productively efficient.

   a. Perfect competition
   b. General equilibrium
   c. Law of supply
   d. Co-operative economics

26. In microeconomics, _____ is quite simply the conversion of inputs into outputs. It is an economic process that uses resources to create a good or service that is suitable for exchange. This can include manufacturing, storing, shipping, and packaging.

   a. Red Guards
   b. Solved
   c. MET
   d. Production

27. _____ is the term denoting either an entrance or changes which are inserted into a system and which activate/modify a process. It is an abstract concept, used in the modeling, system(s) design and system(s) exploitation. It is usually connected with other terms, e.g., _____ field, _____ variable, _____ parameter, _____ value, _____ signal, _____ device and _____ file.

   a. AD-IA Model
   b. ACCRA Cost of Living Index
   c. Input
   d. ACEA agreement

28. In economics, an _____ is a contour line drawn through the set of points at which the same quantity of output is produced while changing the quantities of two or more inputs. While an indifference curve helps to answer the utility-maximizing problem of consumers, the _____ deals with the cost-minimization problem of producers. _____s are typically drawn on capital-labor graphs, showing the tradeoff between capital and labor in the production function, and the decreasing marginal returns of both inputs.

a. Economies of scale

b. Underinvestment employment relationship

c. Economic production quantity

d. Isoquant

29. _____ and behavioral finance are closely related fields that have evolved to be a separate branch of economic and financial analysis which applies scientific research on human and social, cognitive and emotional factors to better understand economic decisions by consumers, borrowers, investors, and how they affect market prices, returns and the allocation of resources.

The field is primarily concerned with the bounds of rationality (selfishness, self-control) of economic agents. Behavioral models typically integrate insights from psychology with neo-classical economic theory.

a. Behavioral economics

b. Mainstream economics

c. Neoclassical economics

d. Georgism

30. In economics an _____ line represents a combination of inputs which all cost the same amount. Although similar to the budget constraint in consumer theory, the use of the _____ pertains to cost-minimization in production, as opposed to utility-maximization. The typical _____ line represents the ratio of costs of labour and capital, so the formula is often written as:

$$rK + wL = C$$

Where w represents the wage of labour, and r represents the rental rate of capital.

a. Incentive

b. Isocost

c. Epstein-Zin preferences

d. Inventory analysis

31. The slope of the production-possibility frontier (PPF) at any given point is called the _____ It describes numerically the rate at which one good can be transformed into the other. It is also called the (marginal) 'opportunity cost' of a commodity, that is, it is the opportunity cost of X in terms of Y at the margin.

a. Productivity

b. Piece work

c. Marginal rate of transformation

d. Fordism

32. In economics, the _____ of a good or of a service is the utility of the specific use to which an agent would put a given increase in that good or service, or of the specific use that would be abandoned in response to a given decrease. In other words, _____ is the utility of the marginal use -- which, on the assumption of economic rationality, would be the least urgent use of the good or service, from the best feasible combination of actions in which its use is included. Under the mainstream assumptions, the _____ of a good or service is the posited quantified change in utility obtained by increasing or by decreasing use of that good or service.

a. 100-year flood

b. 1921 recession

c. 130-30 fund

d. Marginal Utility

33. _____ is a common market structure where many competing producers sell products that are differentiated from one another (ie. the products are substitutes, but are not exactly alike.) Many markets are monopolistically competitive, common examples include the markets for restaurants, cereal, clothing, shoes and service industries in large cities.

a. Financial crisis

b. Perfect competition

c. Monopolistic Competition

d. Mathematical economics

34. In economics, _____ refers to the ability of a party to produce a good or service using fewer real resources than another entity producing the same good or service..A party has an _____ when using the same input as another party, it can produce a greater output. Since _____ is determined by a simple comparison of labor productivities, it is possible for a a party to have no _____ in anything. It can be contrasted with the concept of comparative advantage which refers to the ability to produce a particular good at a lower opportunity cost.

a. International economics

b. Absolute advantage

c. Index number

d. ACCRA Cost of Living Index

35. In economics, _____ refers to the ability of a person or a country to produce a particular good at a lower marginal cost and opportunity cost than another person or country. It is the ability to produce a product most efficiently given all the other products that could be produced. It can be contrasted with absolute advantage which refers to the ability of a person or a country to produce a particular good at a lower absolute cost than another.

a. Comparative advantage

b. Gravity model of trade

c. Hot money

d. Triffin dilemma

36. _____ is a type of trade policy that allows traders to act and transact without interference from government. Thus, the policy permits trading partners mutual gains from trade, with goods and services produced according to the theory of comparative advantage.

Under a _____ policy, prices are a reflection of true supply and demand, and are the sole determinant of resource allocation.

a. 130-30 fund

b. 100-year flood

c. Free trade

d. 1921 recession

37. In economics, an _____ is any good (e.g. a commodity) or service brought into one country from another country in a legitimate fashion, typically for use in trade.It is a good that is brought in from another country for sale. _____ goods or services are provided to domestic consumers by foreign producers. An _____ in the receiving country is an export to the sending country.

a. Incoterms

b. Import quota

c. Economic integration

d. Import

38. An _____ is a type of protectionist trade restriction that sets a physical limit on the quantity of a good that can be imported into a country in a given period of time. Quotas, like other trade restrictions, are used to benefit the producers of a good in a domestic economy at the expense of all consumers of the good in that economy.

Critics say quotas often lead to corruption (bribes to get a quota allocation), smuggling (circumventing a quota), and higher prices for consumers.

a. International Monetary Systems

b. Economic integration

c. Agreement on Agriculture

d. Import quota

39. In economics, an _____ is any good or commodity, transported from one country to another country in a legitimate fashion, typically for use in trade. _____ goods or services are provided to foreign consumers by domestic producers. _____ is an important part of international trade.

a. Export
b. AD-IA Model
c. ACCRA Cost of Living Index
d. ACEA agreement

40. The _____ is a trilateral trade bloc in North America created by the governments of the United States, Canada, and Mexico. The agreement creating the trade bloc came into force on January 1, 1994. It superseded the Canada-United States Free Trade Agreement between the U.S. and Canada.

a. North American Free Trade Agreement
b. Federal Reserve Bank Notes
c. Case-Shiller Home Price Indices
d. Demand-side technologies

41. _____ is the economic policy of restraining trade between states, through methods such as tariffs on imported goods, restrictive quotas, and a variety of other restrictive government regulations designed to discourage imports, and prevent foreign take-over of local markets and companies. This policy is closely aligned with anti-globalization, and contrasts with free trade, where government barriers to trade are kept to a minimum. The term is mostly used in the context of economics, where _____ refers to policies or doctrines which 'protect' businesses and workers within a country by restricting or regulating trade with foreign nations.

a. Google economy
b. Digital economy
c. Protectionism
d. Knowledge economy

42. The term surplus is used in economics for several related quantities. The _____ is the amount that consumers benefit by being able to purchase a product for a price that is less than they would be willing to pay. The producer surplus is the amount that producers benefit by selling at a market price mechanism that is higher than they would be willing to sell for.

a. Marginal rate of technical substitution
b. Consumer surplus
c. Necessity good
d. Microeconomic reform

43. In economics, the _____ or the Technical Rate of Substitution (TRS) is the amount by which the quantity of one input has to be reduced ($-\Delta x_2$) when one extra unit of another input is used ($\Delta x_1 = 1$), so that output remains constant ($y = \bar{y}$.)

$$MRTS(x_1, x_2) = \frac{\Delta x_2}{\Delta x_1} = -\frac{MP_1}{MP_2}$$

where MP_1 and MP_2 are the marginal products of input 1 and input 2, respectively.

Along an isoquant, the MRTS shows the rate at which one input (e.g. capital or labor) may be substituted for another, while maintaining the same level of output.

a. Marginal rate of technical substitution
b. Household production function
c. Pork cycle
d. Producer surplus

44.   In economics, _____ is the process by which a firm determines the price and output level that returns the greatest profit. There are several approaches to this problem. The total revenue--total cost method relies on the fact that profit equals revenue minus cost, and the marginal revenue--marginal cost method is based on the fact that total profit in a perfectly competitive market reaches its maximum point where marginal revenue equals marginal cost.

a. Profit margin   b. Profit maximization
c. 100-year flood   d. Normal profit

45.   In economics, an _____ or spillover of an economic transaction is an impact on a party that is not directly involved in the transaction. In such a case, prices do not reflect the full costs or benefits in production or consumption of a product or service. A positive impact is called an external benefit, while a negative impact is called an external cost.

a. Environmental impact assessment   b. Environmental tariff
c. Existence value   d. Externality

46.   In economics, a _____ exists when the production or use of goods and services by the market is not efficient. That is, there exists another outcome where all involved can be made better off. _____s can be viewed as scenarios where individuals' pursuit of pure self-interest leads to results that are not efficient - that can be improved upon from the societal point-of-view.

a. Market failure   b. Fixed exchange rate
c. General equilibrium   d. Financial economics

47.   In economics, _____ is the ability of a firm to alter the market price of a good or service. A firm with _____ can raise prices without losing all customers to competitors.

When a firm has _____ it faces a downward-sloping demand curve.

a. Pacman conjecture   b. Revenue-cap regulation
c. Price makers   d. Market power

48.   In economics, a _____ exists when a specific individual or enterprise has sufficient control over a particular product or service to determine significantly the terms on which other individuals shall have access to it. Monopolies are thus characterized by a lack of economic competition for the good or service that they provide and a lack of viable substitute goods. The verb 'monopolize' refers to the process by which a firm gains persistently greater market share than what is expected under perfect competition.

a. 130-30 fund   b. 100-year flood
c. 1921 recession   d. Monopoly

49.   In economics, a _____ is a good that is non-rivaled and non-excludable. This means, respectively, that consumption of the good by one individual does not reduce availability of the good for consumption by others; and that no one can be effectively excluded from using the good. In the real world, there may be no such thing as an absolutely non-rivaled and non-excludable good; but economists think that some goods approximate the concept closely enough for the analysis to be economically useful.

a. Public good   b. Happiness economics
c. Neoclassical synthesis   d. Demand-pull theory

50. A _____ is an object whose consumption increases the utility of the consumer, for which the quantity demanded exceeds the quantity supplied at zero price. _____s are usually modeled as having diminishing marginal utility. The first individual purchase has high utility; the second has less.

a. Composite good

b. Good

c. Pie method

d. Merit good

1.   Although information has been bought and sold since ancient times, the idea of an information marketplace is relatively recent. The nature of such markets is still evolving, which complicates development of sustainable business models. However, certain attributes of _____ are beginning to be understood, such as diminished participation costs, opportunities for customization, shifting customer relations, and a need for order.
   a. Intention economy   b. Open economy
   c. Underground economy   d. Information markets

2.   _____, anti-selection insurance, statistics, and risk management. It refers to a market process in which 'bad' results occur when buyers and sellers have asymmetric information (i.e. access to different information): the 'bad' products or customers are more likely to be selected. A bank that sets one price for all its checking account customers runs the risk of being adversely selected against by its low-balance, high-activity (and hence least profitable) customers.
   a. ACCRA Cost of Living Index   b. ACEA agreement
   c. AD-IA Model   d. Adverse selection

3.   _____, in law and economics, is a form of risk management primarily used to hedge against the risk of a contingent loss. _____ is defined as the equitable transfer of the risk of a loss, from one entity to another, in exchange for a premium, and can be thought of as a guaranteed small loss to prevent a large, possibly devastating loss. An insurer is a company selling the _____; an insured or policyholder is the person or entity buying the _____.
   a. ACEA agreement   b. AD-IA Model
   c. ACCRA Cost of Living Index   d. Insurance

4.   _____ describes a deliberate attempt to interfere with the free and fair operation of the market and create artificial, false or misleading appearances with respect to the price of a security, commodity or currency. _____ is prohibited under Section 9(a)(2) of the Securities Exchange Act of 1934, and in Australia under Section s 1041A of the Corporations Act 2001. The Act defines _____ as transactions which create an artificial price or maintain an artificial price for a tradable security.
   a. Market manipulation   b. Managerial economics
   c. Legal monopoly   d. Net domestic product

5.   A _____ refers to any type debt instrument, such as a loan, bond, mortgage that does not have a fixed rate of interest over the life of the instrument. Such debt typically uses an index or other base rate for establishing the interest rate for each relevant period. One of the most common rates to use as the basis for applying interest rates is the London Inter-bank Offered Rate, or LIBOR
   a. Disposal tax effect   b. Moneylender
   c. Money market   d. Floating interest rate

6.   An _____ is quite usually a standard guarantee from the seller of a product that specifies the extent to which the quality or performance of the product is assured and states the conditions under which the product can be returned, replaced, or repaired. It is often given in the form of a specific, written 'Warranty' document. However, a warranty may also arise by operation of law based upon the seller's description of the goods, and perhaps their source and quality, and any material deviation from that specification would violate the guarantee.
   a. ACEA agreement   b. ACCRA Cost of Living Index
   c. Express warranty   d. AD-IA Model

7.   _____ is the prospect that a party insulated from risk may behave differently from the way it would behave if it were fully exposed to the risk. In insurance, _____ that occurs without conscious or malicious action is called morale hazard.

_____ is related to information asymmetry, a situation in which one party in a transaction has more information than another.

a. 100-year flood

b. 130-30 fund

c. 1921 recession

d. Moral hazard

8. In political science and economics, the _____ or agency dilemma treats the difficulties that arise under conditions of incomplete and asymmetric information when a principal hires an agent, such as the problem that the two may not have the same interests, while the principal is, presumably, hiring the agent to pursue the interests of the former.

Various mechanisms may be used to try to align the interests of the agent with those of the principal, such as piece rates/commissions, profit sharing, efficiency wages, performance measurement (including financial statements), the agent posting a bond, or fear of firing. The _____ is found in most employer/employee relationships, for example, when stockholders hire top executives of corporations.

a. Principal-agent problem

b. 1921 recession

c. 100-year flood

d. 130-30 fund

9. This MAD scenario is often referred to as _____. The term deterrence was first used in this context after World War II; prior to that time, its use was limited to legal terminology.

In practice, the theory proved both utterly effective and exceptionally dangerous (e.g., Cuban Missile Crisis) through the end of the Cold War.

a. Mutual assured destruction

b. Nuclear deterrence

c. Berlin Wall

d. Sino-Soviet split

10. The _____ is a Cabinet-level office, and is the largest office within the Executive Office of the President of the United States (EOP.) It is an important conduit by which the White House oversees the activities of federal agencies. OMB is tasked with giving expert advice to senior White House officials on a range of topics relating to federal policy, management, legislative, regulatory, and budgetary issues.

a. ACEA agreement

b. ACCRA Cost of Living Index

c. AD-IA Model

d. Office of Management and Budget

11. To _____ is to impose a financial charge or other levy upon a taxpayer by a state or the functional equivalent of a state.

_____es are also imposed by many subnational entities. _____es consist of direct _____ or indirect _____, and may be paid in money or as its labour equivalent (often but not always unpaid.)

a. 130-30 fund

b. Tax

c. 1921 recession

d. 100-year flood

12. To tax is to impose a financial charge or other levy upon a taxpayer by a state or the functional equivalent of a state.

_____ are also imposed by many subnational entities. _____ consist of direct tax or indirect tax, and may be paid in money or as its labour equivalent (often but not always unpaid.)

   a. 100-year flood   b. Taxes

   c. 1921 recession   d. 130-30 fund

13.   In economics and sociology, an _____ is any factor (financial or non-financial) that enables or motivates a particular course of action, or counts as a reason for preferring one choice to the alternatives. It is an expectation that encourages people to behave in a certain way. Since human beings are purposeful creatures, the study of _____ structures is central to the study of all economic activity (both in terms of individual decision-making and in terms of co-operation and competition within a larger institutional structure.)

   a. Incentive   b. Isocost

   c. Economic reform   d. Epstein-Zin preferences

14.   In labor economics, the _____ hypothesis argues that wages, at least in some markets, are determined by more than simply supply and demand. Specifically, it points to the incentive for managers to pay their employees more than the market-clearing wage in order to increase their productivity or efficiency. This increased labor productivity pays for the relatively higher wages.

   a. Efficiency wage   b. Earnings calls

   c. Exogenous growth model   d. Inflatable rats

15.   In economics, the _____ is the wage rate that produces neither an access supply of workers nor an excess demand for workers and labor market. See economic equilibrium.

   a. Effective unemployment rate   b. International free trade agreement

   c. Equilibrium wage   d. Economic stability

16.   _____ was the American founder of the Ford Motor Company and father of modern assembly lines used in mass production. His introduction of the Model T automobile revolutionized transportation and American industry. He was a prolific inventor and was awarded 161 U.S. patents.

   a. Henry Ford   b. George Cabot Lodge II

   c. Maximilian Carl Emil Weber   d. Werner Sombart

1. In economics, an _____ or spillover of an economic transaction is an impact on a party that is not directly involved in the transaction. In such a case, prices do not reflect the full costs or benefits in production or consumption of a product or service. A positive impact is called an external benefit, while a negative impact is called an external cost.
    a. Externality
    c. Environmental tariff
    b. Existence value
    d. Environmental impact assessment

2. Many _____ are related to the environmental consequences of production and use

    - Systemic risk describes the risks to the overall economy arising from the risks which the banking system takes. That the private costs of banking failure may be smaller than the social costs justifies banking regulations, although regulations could create a moral hazard.

    - Anthropogenic climate change is attributed to greenhouse gas emissions from burning oil, gas, and coal. Global warming has been ranked as the #1 externality of all economic activity, in the magnitude of potential harms and yet remains unmitigated.

    a. Green certificate
    c. Total Economic Value
    b. White certificates
    d. Negative externalities

3. In economics and finance, _____ is the change in total cost that arises when the quantity produced changes by one unit. It is the cost of producing one more unit of a good. Mathematically, the _____ function is expressed as the first derivative of the total cost (TC) function with respect to quantity (Q.)
    a. Marginal cost
    c. Variable cost
    b. Khozraschyot
    d. Quality costs

4. In economics _____ is defined as the sum of private and external costs. Economic theorists ascribe individual decision-making to a calculation costs and benefits. Rational choice theory assumes that individuals only consider their own private costs when making decisions, not the costs that may be borne by others.
    a. Psychic cost
    c. Cost-Volume-Profit Analysis
    b. Social cost
    d. Khozraschyot

5. Examples of _____ include:

- A beekeeper keeps the bees for their honey. A side effect or externality associated with his activity is the pollination of surrounding crops by the bees. The value generated by the pollination may be more important than the value of the harvested honey.

- An individual planting an attractive garden in front of his house may provide benefits to others living in the area, and even financial benefits in the form of increased property values for all property owners.

- An individual buying a product that is interconnected in a network (e.g., a video cellphone) will increase the usefulness of such phones to other people who have a video cellphone. When each new user of a product increases the value of the same product owned by others, the phenomenon is called a network externality or a network effect. Network externalities often have 'tipping points' where, suddenly, the product reaches general acceptance and near-universal usage, a phenomenon which can be seen in the near universal take-up of cellphones in some Scandinavian countries.

- Knowledge spillover of inventions and information - once an invention (or most other forms of practical information) is discovered or made more easily accessible, others benefit by exploiting the invention or information. Copyright and intellectual property law are mechanisms to allow the inventor or creator to benefit from a temporary, state-protected monopoly in return for 'sharing' the information through publication or other means.

a. Positive externalities   b. Negative externalities
c. Total Economic Value   d. Weighted average cost of carbon

6. In economics, an externality or spillover of an economic transaction is an impact on a party that is not directly involved in the transaction. In such a case, prices do not reflect the full costs or benefits in production or consumption of a product or service. A positive impact is called an _____, while a negative impact is called an external cost.
a. External benefit   b. ACCRA Cost of Living Index
c. ACEA agreement   d. AD-IA Model

7. In economics, a _____ exists when the production or use of goods and services by the market is not efficient. That is, there exists another outcome where all involved can be made better off. _____s can be viewed as scenarios where individuals' pursuit of pure self-interest leads to results that are not efficient - that can be improved upon from the societal point-of-view.
a. Market failure   b. Financial economics
c. General equilibrium   d. Fixed exchange rate

8. Under the system of feudalism, a _____, fief, feud, feoff often consisted of inheritable lands or revenue-producing property granted by a liege lord, generally to a vassal, in return for a form of allegiance, originally to give him the means to fulfill his military duties when called upon. However anything of value could be held in fief, such as an office, a right of exploitation (e.g., hunting, fishing) or any other type of revenue, rather than the land it comes from.

Originally, the feudal institution of vassalage did not imply the giving or receiving of landholdings (which were granted only as a reward for loyalty), but by the eighth century the giving of a landholding was becoming standard.

a. Fiefdom

b. 130-30 fund

c. 100-year flood

d. 1921 recession

9.   In microeconomics, _____ is quite simply the conversion of inputs into outputs. It is an economic process that uses resources to create a good or service that is suitable for exchange. This can include manufacturing, storing, shipping, and packaging.

a. MET

b. Red Guards

c. Solved

d. Production

10.   In economics, a _____ is a function that specifies the output of a firm, an industry, or an entire economy for all combinations of inputs. A meta-_____ compares the practice of the existing entities converting inputs X into output y to determine the most efficient practice _____ of the existing entities, whether the most efficient feasible practice production or the most efficient actual practice production. In either case, the maximum output of a technologically-determined production process is a mathematical function of input factors of production.

a. Post-Fordism

b. Constant elasticity of substitution

c. Short-run

d. Production function

11.   _____ is a practice of protecting the environment, on individual, organisational or governmental level, for the benefit of the natural environment and (or) humans.

Due to the pressures of population and technology the biophysical environment is being degraded, sometimes permanently. This has been recognised and governments began placing restraints on activities that caused environmental degradation.

a. AD-IA Model

b. ACEA agreement

c. ACCRA Cost of Living Index

d. Environmental Protection

12.   _____ is an administrative approach used to control pollution by providing economic incentives for achieving reductions in the emissions of pollutants. It is sometimes called cap and trade. A coal power plant in Germany.

a. International Climate Science Coalition

b. ACCRA Cost of Living Index

c. Efficient energy use

d. Emissions trading

13.   In economics, an _____ is any good (e.g. a commodity) or service brought into one country from another country in a legitimate fashion, typically for use in trade.It is a good that is brought in from another country for sale. _____ goods or services are provided to domestic consumers by foreign producers. An _____ in the receiving country is an export to the sending country.

a. Import

b. Import quota

c. Incoterms

d. Economic integration

14.   An _____ is a type of protectionist trade restriction that sets a physical limit on the quantity of a good that can be imported into a country in a given period of time. Quotas, like other trade restrictions, are used to benefit the producers of a good in a domestic economy at the expense of all consumers of the good in that economy.

Critics say quotas often lead to corruption (bribes to get a quota allocation), smuggling (circumventing a quota), and higher prices for consumers.

a. Economic integration   b. Agreement on Agriculture

c. International Monetary Systems   d. Import quota

15. _____ in economics and business is the result of an exchange and from that trade we assign a numerical monetary value to a good, service or asset. If Alice trades Bob 4 apples for an orange, the _____ of an orange is 4 apples. Inversely, the _____ of an apple is 1/4 oranges.

a. Price war   b. Premium pricing

c. Price book   d. Price

16. _____ involves processing used materials into new products in order to prevent waste of potentially useful materials, reduce the consumption of fresh raw materials, reduce energy usage, reduce air pollution (from incineration) and water pollution (from landfilling) by reducing the need for 'conventional' waste disposal, and lower greenhouse gas emissions as compared to virgin production. _____ is a key component of modern waste management and is the third component of the 'Reduce, Reuse, Recycle' waste hierarchy.

Recyclable materials include many kinds of glass, paper, metal, plastic, textiles, and electronics.

a. Recycling   b. 2008 budget crisis

c. Cash or share options   d. History of minimum wage

17. A municipality is an administrative entity composed of a clearly defined territory and its population and commonly denotes a city, town or a small grouping of them. A municipality is typically governed by a mayor and a city council or _____ council.

The notion of municipality includes townships but is not restricted to them.

a. 100-year flood   b. 130-30 fund

c. Municipal   d. 1921 recession

18. _____s is the social science that studies the production, distribution, and consumption of goods and services. The term _____s comes from the Ancient Greek oá¼°κονομῑα from oá¼¶κος (oikos, 'house') + vΪŒμος (nomos, 'custom' or 'law'), hence 'rules of the house(hold)'. Current _____ models developed out of the broader field of political economy in the late 19th century, owing to a desire to use an empirical approach more akin to the physical sciences.

a. Opportunity cost   b. Energy economics

c. Inflation   d. Economic

19. _____ is used to refer to a number of related concepts. It is the using resources in such a way as to maximize the production of goods and services. A system can be called economically efficient if:

- No one can be made better off without making someone else worse off.
- More output cannot be obtained without increasing the amount of inputs.
- Production proceeds at the lowest possible per-unit cost.

These definitions of efficiency are not equivalent, but they are all encompassed by the idea that nothing more can be achieved given the resources available.

An economic system is more efficient if it can provide more goods and services for society without using more resources.

a. ACCRA Cost of Living Index

b. ACEA agreement

c. Economic efficiency

d. Efficient contract theory

20. A _____ is the exclusive authority to determine how a resource is used, whether that resource is owned by government or by individuals. All economic goods have a _____s attribute. This attribute has three broad components

1. The right to use the good
2. The right to earn income from the good
3. The right to transfer the good to others

The concept of _____s as used by economists and legal scholars are related but distinct. The distinction is largely seen in the economists' focus on the ability of an individual or collective to control the use of the good.

a. Post-sale restraint

b. Property right

c. High-reeve

d. Holder in due course

21. In economics, and cost accounting, _____ describes the total economic cost of production and is made up of variable costs, which vary according to the quantity of a good produced and include inputs such as labor and raw materials, plus fixed costs, which are independent of the quantity of a good produced and include inputs (capital) that cannot be varied in the short term, such as buildings and machinery. _____ in economics includes the total opportunity cost of each factor of production in addition to fixed and variable costs.

The rate at which _____ changes as the amount produced changes is called marginal cost.

a. 1921 recession

b. Total cost

c. 130-30 fund

d. 100-year flood

22. In law and economics, the _____, describes the economic efficiency of an economic allocation or outcome in the presence of externalities. The theorem states that when trade in an externality is possible and there are no transaction costs, bargaining will lead to an efficient outcome regardless of the initial allocation of property rights. In practice, obstacles to bargaining or poorly defined property rights can prevent Coasian bargaining.

a. Means test

b. Prior appropriation water rights

c. General Mining Act of 1872

d. Coase theorem

23. A _____ is a public market for the trading of company stock and derivatives at an agreed price; these are securities listed on a stock exchange as well as those only traded privately.

The size of the world _____ was estimated at about $36.6 trillion US at the beginning of October 2008 . The total world derivatives market has been estimated at about $791 trillion face or nominal value, 11 times the size of the entire world economy.

a. Adolf Hitler   b. Adam Smith

c. Adolph Fischer   d. Stock market

24.   In economics, a common-pool resource, alternatively termed a _____ resource, is a particular type of good consisting of a natural or human-made resource system, the size or characteristics of which makes it costly, but not impossible, to exclude potential beneficiaries from obtaining benefits from its use. Unlike pure public goods, common pool resources face problems of congestion or overuse, because they are subtractable. A common-pool resource typically consists of a core resource, which defines the stock variable, while providing a limited quantity of extractable fringe units, which defines the flow variable.

a. Price-cap regulation   b. Common property

c. Common-pool resource   d. Government monopoly

25.   In economics, a _____ is a good that is non-rivaled and non-excludable. This means, respectively, that consumption of the good by one individual does not reduce availability of the good for consumption by others; and that no one can be effectively excluded from using the good. In the real world, there may be no such thing as an absolutely non-rivaled and non-excludable good; but economists think that some goods approximate the concept closely enough for the analysis to be economically useful.

a. Demand-pull theory   b. Public good

c. Happiness economics   d. Neoclassical synthesis

26.   A _____ is an object whose consumption increases the utility of the consumer, for which the quantity demanded exceeds the quantity supplied at zero price. _____s are usually modeled as having diminishing marginal utility. The first individual purchase has high utility; the second has less.

a. Composite good   b. Merit good

c. Good   d. Pie method

27.   Economics:

- _____,the desire to own something and the ability to pay for it
- _____ curve,a graphic representation of a _____ schedule
- _____ deposit, the money in checking accounts
- _____ pull theory,the theory that inflation occurs when _____ for goods and services exceeds existing supplies
- _____ schedule,a table that lists the quantity of a good a person will buy it each different price
- _____ side economics,the school of economics at believes government spending and tax cuts open economy by raising _____

a. McKesson ' Robbins scandal   b. Production

c. Variability   d. Demand

28.   _____ is the observation that people often do and believe things because many other people do and believe the same things. The effect is often pejoratively called herding instinct, particularly when applied to adolescents. People tend to follow the crowd without examining the merits of a particular thing.

a. Bandwagon effect

b. Halo effect

c. Hyperbolic discounting

d. Sunk costs

29.   In statistics, _____ is used for two things;

- to construct a simple formula that will predict a value or values for a variable given the value of another variable.
- to test whether and how a given variable is related to another variable or variables.

Note: correlation does not imply causation.

_____ is a form of regression analysis in which the relationship between one or more independent variables and another variable, called the dependent variable, is modelled by a least squares function, called a _____ equation. This function is a linear combination of one or more model parameters, called regression coefficients. A _____ equation with one independent variable represents a straight line when the predicted value (i.e. the dependant variable from the regression equation) is plotted against the independent variable: this is called a simple _____.

a. Mathematical statistics

b. Polynomial regression

c. Nonlinear regression

d. Linear regression

30.   In statistics, _____ refers to techniques for the modeling and analysis of numerical data consisting of values of a dependent variable and of one or more independent variables The dependent variable in the regression equation is modeled as a function of the independent variables, corresponding parameters, and an error term. The error term is treated as a random variable.

a. 100-year flood

b. 130-30 fund

c. 1921 recession

d. Regression analysis

31.   In statistics, _____ has two related meanings:

- the arithmetic _____
- the expected value of a random variable, which is also called the population _____.

It is sometimes stated that the '_____' _____s average. This is incorrect if '_____' is taken in the specific sense of 'arithmetic _____' as there are different types of averages: the _____, median, and mode. Other simple statistical analyses use measures of spread, such as range, interquartile range, or standard deviation. For a real-valued random variable X, the _____ is the expectation of X. Note that not every probability distribution has a defined _____ (or variance); see the Cauchy distribution for an example.

a. 100-year flood

b. Mean

c. 1921 recession

d. 130-30 fund

32.   In mathematics, a _____ is a constant multiplicative factor of a certain object. For example, in the expression $9x^2$, the _____ of x^2 is 9.

The object can be such things as a variable, a vector, a function, etc.

a. Coefficient   b. 130-30 fund
c. 1921 recession   d. 100-year flood

33.   In statistics, a _____ is an interval estimate of a population parameter. Instead of estimating the parameter by a single value, an interval likely to include the parameter is given. Thus, _____s are used to indicate the reliability of an estimate.

a. Logistic regression   b. Biostatistics
c. Polynomial regression   d. Confidence interval

34.   In statistics, a _____ is, broadly speaking, a statistic whose sampling distribution is a Student's t-distribution. These are a parametric statistic, most frequently used in frequentist statistical hypothesis testing in Student's t-tests, but can be defined and used independently of hypothesis testing.

Broadly speaking, a _____ is any statistic whose sampling distribution is a Student's t-distribution.

a. Path coefficients   b. T-statistic
c. Kurtosis risk   d. Standardized coefficients

35.   _____ is the process of making predictions about the economy as a whole or in part.

Relevant models include

- Economic base analysis
- Shift-share analysis
- Input-output model
- Grinold and Kroner Model

.

a. Overproduction   b. Investment goods
c. Australian Financial Services Licence   d. Economic forecasting

36.   The term _____ is a neo-Latin word meaning 'before the event'. _____ is used most commonly in the commercial world, where results of a particular action, or series of actions, are forecast in advance. The opposite of _____ is ex-post .

a. AD-IA Model   b. ACCRA Cost of Living Index
c. ACEA agreement   d. Ex-ante

37.   _____ is the process of estimation in unknown situations. Prediction is a similar, but more general term. Both can refer to estimation of time series, cross-sectional or longitudinal data.

a. 1921 recession   b. 130-30 fund
c. 100-year flood   d. Forecasting

Chapter 1

1. d	2. b	3. d	4. d	5. d	6. c	7. d	8. b	9. b	10. a
11. a	12. a	13. d	14. d	15. a	16. b	17. d	18. d	19. d	20. c
21. d	22. d	23. d	24. b	25. d	26. c	27. d	28. d	29. c	

Chapter 2

1. b	2. d	3. b	4. c	5. b	6. d	7. d	8. c	9. d	10. d
11. b	12. b	13. d	14. d	15. b	16. d	17. b	18. a	19. d	20. b
21. d	22. c	23. d	24. d	25. a	26. d	27. d	28. b	29. b	30. c

Chapter 3

1. d	2. a	3. d	4. a	5. d	6. c	7. d	8. b	9. d	10. c
11. d	12. d	13. c	14. d	15. d	16. a	17. d	18. c	19. d	20. a
21. a	22. a	23. d	24. a	25. a	26. a	27. b	28. d	29. d	30. d
31. d									

Chapter 4

1. c	2. d	3. d	4. d	5. a	6. d	7. d	8. d	9. d	10. b
11. d	12. d	13. a	14. d	15. d	16. b	17. d	18. d	19. d	20. a
21. d	22. d	23. d	24. a	25. c	26. a	27. c	28. d	29. d	30. b
31. a	32. b	33. c	34. b						

Chapter 5

1. d	2. a	3. d	4. c	5. d	6. d	7. c	8. d	9. d	10. c
11. c	12. a	13. a	14. d	15. a	16. d	17. a	18. d	19. d	20. c
21. b	22. b	23. d	24. d	25. d	26. d	27. d	28. a	29. b	30. b
31. d									

Chapter 6

1. b	2. b	3. d	4. d	5. c	6. c	7. c	8. d	9. d	10. d
11. d	12. d	13. d	14. d	15. d	16. b	17. c	18. d	19. d	

Chapter 7

1. c	2. d	3. d	4. c	5. a	6. d	7. b	8. c	9. d	10. d
11. d	12. d	13. a	14. a	15. b	16. d	17. c	18. d	19. b	20. d
21. d	22. a	23. b	24. a	25. a	26. c	27. d	28. a	29. c	30. b
31. d	32. a	33. d	34. b	35. c	36. c	37. d	38. d		

Chapter 8

1. b	2. a	3. d	4. d	5. d	6. a	7. b	8. a	9. b	10. a
11. d	12. a	13. d	14. d	15. c	16. d	17. d	18. d	19. d	20. a
21. a	22. d	23. a	24. d	25. d	26. d	27. b	28. d	29. d	30. a
31. d	32. d	33. b	34. c	35. d	36. d				

Chapter 9

1. d	2. c	3. c	4. d	5. c	6. d	7. d	8. b	9. d	10. a
11. d	12. d	13. c	14. d	15. b	16. c	17. a	18. d	19. a	20. b
21. d	22. a	23. a	24. c	25. d	26. d	27. d	28. d	29. c	30. d
31. d	32. c	33. b							

Chapter 10

1. a	2. a	3. d	4. c	5. d	6. b	7. d	8. b	9. b	10. d
11. c	12. a	13. d	14. d	15. b	16. d	17. c	18. d	19. d	20. b
21. b	22. d	23. c	24. b	25. c	26. a	27. d	28. a	29. d	30. d
31. b	32. b	33. d	34. d	35. d	36. d	37. a	38. d	39. c	40. d
41. a	42. b	43. b							

Chapter 11

1. d	2. d	3. d	4. b	5. c	6. d	7. d	8. d	9. d	10. d
11. a	12. a	13. a	14. d	15. d	16. d	17. d	18. b	19. d	20. c
21. d	22. b	23. d	24. d	25. d	26. b				

Chapter 12

1. b	2. b	3. a	4. d	5. a	6. c	7. d	8. d	9. a	10. a
11. d	12. d	13. d	14. d	15. b	16. a	17. d	18. d	19. d	20. a
21. d	22. d	23. d	24. d	25. a	26. a	27. b	28. d	29. d	30. b

Chapter 13

1. a	2. d	3. c	4. d	5. b	6. d	7. d	8. d	9. d	10. b
11. a	12. d	13. d	14. d	15. b	16. d	17. c	18. b	19. c	

Chapter 14

1. d	2. a	3. a	4. d	5. d	6. c	7. d	8. d	9. d	10. d
11. d	12. d	13. b	14. d	15. a	16. d	17. d	18. d	19. c	20. d
21. b	22. a	23. d	24. b	25. d	26. d	27. b	28. d	29. a	30. d

Chapter 15

1. b	2. a	3. d	4. d	5. a	6. a	7. a	8. b	9. d	10. d
11. d	12. d	13. b	14. c	15. a	16. a	17. d	18. b	19. d	20. c
21. d	22. a	23. d	24. d	25. c	26. b	27. b	28. d	29. d	30. a
31. d	32. d	33. d	34. d	35. c	36. d	37. b	38. d	39. a	40. b
41. b	42. b	43. c	44. c						

Chapter 16

1. d	2. b	3. d	4. d	5. a	6. a	7. d	8. b	9. d	10. d
11. c	12. d	13. b	14. d	15. d	16. a	17. b	18. b	19. d	20. d
21. b	22. a	23. b	24. b	25. a	26. d	27. c	28. d	29. a	30. b
31. c	32. d	33. c	34. b	35. a	36. c	37. d	38. d	39. a	40. a
41. c	42. b	43. a	44. b	45. d	46. a	47. d	48. d	49. a	50. b

Chapter 17

1. d	2. d	3. d	4. a	5. d	6. c	7. d	8. a	9. b	10. d
11. b	12. b	13. a	14. a	15. c	16. a				

Chapter 18

1. a	2. d	3. a	4. b	5. a	6. a	7. a	8. a	9. d	10. d
11. d	12. d	13. a	14. d	15. d	16. a	17. c	18. d	19. c	20. b
21. b	22. d	23. d	24. b	25. b	26. c	27. d	28. a	29. d	30. d
31. b	32. a	33. d	34. b	35. d	36. d	37. d			

9 781428 871878